MW00488336

RETURN OF THE VIKINGS

RETURN OF THE VIKINGS

NORDIC LEADERSHIP IN TIMES OF EXTREME CHANGE

CHRIS SHERN & HENRIK JEBERG
WITH RICHARD MARTIN

Chris Shern & Henrik Jeberg in cooperation with Richard Martin
Return of the Vikings – *Nordic Leadership in Times of
Extreme Change*
© 2018 Chris Shern, Henrik Jeberg & Danish Psychological
Publishers

First published in Denmark by Danish Psychological Publishers A/S.

Publishing editor: Sidsel Fabech
Graphic design and layout: Lea Rathnov/Hofdamerne
Cover: Harvey Macaulay/Imperiet

First Edition 2018
ISBN 978-87-7158-586-5

BoD–Books on Demand/IngramSpark
Printed in Germany 2018/Worldwide (Print on Demand)

Danish Psychological Publishers A/S
Knabrostraede 3, 1.
DK-1210 Copenhagen K
Denmark
www.dpf.dk

All rights reserved. No part of this book may be reproduced or
transmitted in any form or by any means, electronic or mechanical, including photocopying and recording, or in any information
storage or retrieval system without the prior written permission of
Danish Psychological Publishers.

CONTENTS

Foreword 7
Interviewees 9
Nine Noble Virtues 11
Preface 15

PART I ROOTS
Chapter 1 Nordic Views 23
Chapter 2 Viking 45

PART II VIKING VIRTUES
Chapter 3 Courage 61
Chapter 4 Truth 77
Chapter 5 Honor 93
Chapter 6 Fidelity 109
Chapter 7 Discipline 125
Chapter 8 Hospitality 141
Chapter 9 Self-reliance 155
Chapter 10 Industriousness 171
Chapter 11 Perseverance 187

PART III UNCERTAINTY
Chapter 12 Times of Extreme Change 203

About the interviewees 211
Bibliography 231
Filmography 243
Annex: The Inside–Outside Perspective 245
About the Authors 253

FOREWORD

Culturally, politically, philosophically, the Nordic countries and territories have been at the forefront of much that is new and interesting in the Western world. Trendsetters in design, gastronomy, literature and visual art, the Nordics also draw attention today for their business practices and involvement in key international organizations. At an individual, corporate and societal level, the Nordics are gaining recognition for their distinct approach to leadership, as well as for contributions to the global community that are disproportionate to their relatively small size.

As explorers, navigators and political and educational innovators, the Nordic peoples have a rich heritage. This provides deep roots, traced back to the Viking era and before. Nine noble virtues can be derived from Norse mythology and applied in a modern, secular context. This heritage still informs how people in these northern nations live and work today. The global nature of business and communication in the twenty-first century means that the Nordic influence extends well beyond northern Europe. Their methods, values and leadership practices are woven into the DNA of international businesses founded in Denmark, Finland, Iceland, Norway and Sweden, as well as in autonomous territories like Greenland. They are also exemplified by many Nordic practitioners who have chosen to work in other countries or for multinational organizations.

With this book we offer an outsider-on-the-inside and insider-on-the-outside perspective on Nordic leadership. As an American based in Denmark and a Dane based in the United States we have extensive experience working with Nordic organizations around the globe. In the following pages, our own stories are interwoven with those of a diverse range of interviewees, including business executives, entrepreneurs, activists, politicians, restaurateurs and athletes. These stories bring into focus some of the characteristics and behaviors that we associate with Nordic leadership.

Copenhagen and California, April 2018
Chris Shern and Henrik Jeberg

INTERVIEWEES

The authors would like to express their thanks to the numerous people who gave up their time to be interviewed for the *Return of the Vikings* project, either meeting in person or conversing online. Their stories and insights brought to life the behaviors and characteristics associated with Nordic leadership. This book could not have been written without their inspiration and support.

Adiba Barney
Ally Jiang
Anders Fogh Rasmussen
Annelise Goldstein
Birgitta Jónsdóttir
Carmen Sanz
Claus Meyer
Esko Kilpi
Even Bratberg
Friðrik Bjarnason
Heini Zachariassen
Humphrey Lau
Jan Carlzon
Jan Olaf Mirko Härter
Jens W. Moberg
Jo Ashman
Jón Baldvin Hannibalsson
Jon Krogh
Jørgen Lindegaard
Kenneth Mikkelsen
Kigge Hvid
Lars Tvede
Lene Rachel Andersen

Marco Sammicheli
Massimo Caiazza
Melanie McCall
Mika Anttonen
Mikael Kretz
Morten Andersen
Morten Ravn
Niclas Carlsson
Niels Dalhoff
Patrick Trancu
Per Heggenes
Per Tryding
Pernille Hippe Brun
Rasmus Stuhr Jakobsen
Roberto Maiorana
Rufus Gifford
Sakari Oramo
Sanna Suvanto-Harsaae
Stefan Skantz
Thomas Pedersen
Vagn Sørensen
Vincent F. Hendricks
Åslaug Marie Haga

NINE NOBLE VIRTUES

 Courage can be defined as the ability to confront fear, pain, danger, uncertainty or intimidation. It can be divided into *physical courage*—in face of physical pain, hardship and threat of death—and *moral courage*—in the face of shame, scandal and discouragement. In our modern world where only a few of us ever serve as warriors, courage can also mean exposing wrongful practices as a *whistle-blower*, or fighting against racism, sexism, misogyny etc.

 Truth is the state of being in accordance with fact or reality. It is sincerity in action, character and utterance. Having the quality of being free from pretense, deceit or hypocrisy. Being honest to one's self and to others. One who is without truth can never be trusted.

Honor is associated with a keen sense of ethical conduct which allows one to be regarded with great respect and esteem. A quality of worthiness and respectability that affects one's social standing amongst kin and kindred. It is the regard of one's worth and stature based on the harmony of one's actions.

 Fidelity/Trust is defined as the faithfulness to a person, cause or belief which is demonstrated by continual loyalty, trust and support. To never turn one's back and remain complete and undivided. To keep one's word under all circumstances. The quality of being faithful and maintaining a firm adherence to one's own moral values. Fidelity is an ancestor of the word *trust* and is used in synonym throughout the interviews.

 Discipline is associated with the suppression of base desires by restraint and self-control. When an individual uses reason to determine the best course of action regardless of their own personal desires, which may be the opposite of what needs to be done. To stay the course and have the strength to stick to what must be done, even when you don't want to.

 Hospitality is defined as the relationship between a guest and a host, where the host receives the guest with goodwill. This includes the reception and entertainment of guests, visitors or strangers. Hospitality includes a notion of protection. A host not only provides food and shelter to their guest, but also makes sure they do not come to harm while under their care.

 Self-reliance is the state of reliance on oneself or one's own powers and resources by not requiring any aid, support or interaction of others for survival. Self-reliance is the state of personal independence.

 Industriousness is working energetically and devotedly to complete a task or in life's daily toils in a hard-working and diligent manner. Being careful and persistent in one's work or effort. Not being lazy, but having great care in the steadfast application in one's work and effort. Having a sense of industry and a strong work ethic.

 Perseverance is described as the steady persistence in a course of action or purpose. To never give up or surrender, especially in the face of difficulties, obstacles or discouragement. To try and try again until you get it done. Not losing heart and simply giving up or taking the easy way out.

PREFACE

One brand takes fire from another, until it is consumed,
a flame's kindled by flame;
one man becomes clever by talking with another,
but foolish through being reserved.
~ *The Poetic Edda*, Sayings of the High One, Stanza 57

The fact of being an underdog can *change* people in
ways we often fail to appreciate: it can open doors
and create opportunities and educate and enlighten
and make possible what might otherwise have seemed
unthinkable.
~ Malcolm Gladwell, *David and Goliath*

It is the evening of 27 June 2016. In the Stade de Nice, France,
a group of soccer players and coaching staff are gathered near
one of the corner flags. They face the ranked masses of their
impassioned fans. The blue uniforms that adorn players and followers alike indicate that the post-match celebrations are being
conducted by the Icelandic national team and their supporters.

There is another giveaway, which has drawn the admiring attention of both the media and soccer enthusiasts from around the world during the course of UEFA's Euro 2016 tournament.

Everyone in this corner of the stadium, in the stands and on the pitch, has raised their hands in the air. To the increasingly rapid beat of a drum, the hands are clapped, each clap accompanied by a guttural cry. *Huh!* Initially, each cry is followed by a period of silence until the pace becomes so fast that it creates a wall of sound. The shape of the stadium has an amplifying effect. Even filtered via radio and television, it makes a significant impression. For some, at the grounds where the Icelandic team has played its matches, its effects are visceral.

Nicknamed the Viking thunderclap, the "Huh" has become the soundtrack to Iceland's unprecedented progress in an international soccer tournament. What makes the clap so compelling is not that the fans clap in coordinated unison but that they are silent together. Their silence honors the players on the pitch, and it establishes a solidarity between the individual and the community that surrounds them. The silence creates small pockets of reflection, which soon give way to the fevered celebration with which the "Huh" climaxes.

This is Viking heritage reclaimed. The "Huh" connects the modern fans to their medieval forebears, while also serving as the rallying call of a nation accustomed to playing the role of the gritty underdog. Iceland, with a population numbering around 330,000, is one of the smallest nations ever to appear in a major soccer finals round. Earlier in the competition, it was estimated that around a third of the country's population was then in France, one of the largest assemblies ever of Icelanders outside their own country. Now, the national team has just defeated

England for the first time, knocking them out of the tournament, and progressing to the quarter-finals where they will face the host nation. There is cause for celebration.

Iceland's victory is both a beginning and an ending. This is a singular achievement, taking the country into previously uncharted territory. It is also the culmination of a lengthy journey that has legacy thinking at its roots, an outlook requiring adaptive action in the present, always with the objective of future fruition and long-term gain. This has entailed the investment of a financial windfall from television rights in the grassroots of Icelandic soccer, with an emphasis placed on the development of facilities and coaching skills. It has also been witness to a master–apprentice relationship in the leadership of the national team, with the Swede Lars Lagerbäck working alongside and mentoring his Icelandic successor Heimir Hallgrímson.

Nordic people are shaped by the harsh environments they inhabit. Iceland is a volcanic island located on the Mid-Atlantic Ridge where the Eurasian and North American tectonic plates meet. In this sense, it is both of Europe and of America, yet of neither place. The region remains geologically active, subject to the movements of the Earth, the force of the seas and the wintry blanket that envelops it for extended periods each year. Such an environment establishes a certain spirit and fortitude, as well as an existential acceptance that, confronted with the ever-shifting forces of nature, there is always something bigger and more powerful than you. By necessity, Icelanders and the other Nordic peoples are responsive and adaptive. Their survival depends on it.

The allure of the underdog, the archetypal story of David against Goliath, has a strong appeal not only in Iceland but in all the Nordic nations. Individually and collectively, these are small countries whose role and international influence belie the modest size of their populations. Not only in sport but in the political domain, in relation to equality and human rights, in education, in art and design, in science and innovation, in popular culture and cuisine. Norse mythology of the Viking era, documented in Iceland in the form of the *Edda* and the sagas, is filled with stories of anthropomorphic gods getting the better of giants. The taking on of something bigger than oneself is a fact of life in the Nordics. Whether it is a farmer or fisherman confronted with an unpredictable environment, Nordic businesses competing in global markets, Iceland assuming the David-like role in the Cod Wars dispute with the United Kingdom, or each of the Nordic nations fulfilling roles in international communities and organizations, the story scales from the personal to the global.

Life in a Nordic nation like Iceland forges a certain outlook and mindset. This includes an acceptance that anything can happen, a phlegmatic attitude regarding adversity, a willingness to constantly adapt to contextual changes and an ability to put an array of alternative plans into effect when required. The compelling mixture of stoicism and responsiveness is ideally suited to the field of sporting endeavor. But it has resonance beyond the whitewash that marks out the field of play. It is why those in the stands can feel a connection to the exploits of their heroes in Iceland's soccer team. Whether in adversity or triumph, their actions mirror the experiences of the fans themselves. The individual is reflected in the collective and vice versa.

This establishes a strong communal bond. It underpins the positive nationalism that manifested itself so joyously during the Euro 2016 tournament. Far from the xenophobia and fear of otherness that characterizes alt-right political rhetoric, the Nordic pride in their societies is a statement of shared roots and values, a common history and cultural heritage. Present in the moment, but bridging the past and the future, the Icelandic crowd in the Nice stadium signal a connection to their ancestors. With each cry of *Huh*, they celebrate the realization of a long-term plan and proclaim a *Return of the Vikings*.

PART I
ROOTS

CHAPTER 1

NORDIC VIEWS

Do you know how to carve, do you know how
to interpret,
do you know how to color, do you know how
to question,
do you know how to ask, do you know how
to sacrifice,
do you know how to dispatch, do you know how
to slaughter?
~ *The Poetic Edda*, Sayings of the High One, Stanza 144

First, it is learned by doing. We cannot be taught the
virtues. They are habits of thought and action, and the
only way to gain them is to go out and try to do virtuous things. Eventually a habit is formed, and virtue
becomes our new nature. Second, virtue is infectious;
it can become endemic to a place. Our virtuous actions
don't just shape us; they shape society around us by

helping to produce a tradition in which such behavior becomes meaningful and common. The more people who govern their own actions by a particular virtue, the more it becomes a norm that governs others.

~ Ian Goldin & Chris Kutarna, *The Age of Discovery*

It is May 2017. Henrik Jeberg is in the international departure lounge at Copenhagen Airport waiting to board a transatlantic flight to San Francisco. In the cacophony of sound that is the feature of any airport, he finds himself tuning in to the conversation of one particular business traveler. This man is engaged in a short but precise conversation with a colleague back at the office. "You'll find a solution! You have a free hand to solve this. Whatever you come up with I'll adjust my plans accordingly when I land. Bye." Trust, autonomy, adaptiveness. Yet another example of Nordic leadership in action.

The topic is one that has preoccupied us for many years. It has led us to go deeper, following our curiosity about the characteristics and behaviors associated with Nordic leadership both at home and abroad. As a Dane based in California's wine country and an American based in Copenhagen, together we offer an insider-on-the-outside and outsider-on-the-inside perspective. In Chris's case, he has lived Nordic leadership for much of his adult life. In Henrik's case, it is his birthright, experienced during his own school days, practiced in fatherhood and business. It is something he always carries with him, regardless of where he finds himself around the globe.

Chris was born in rural Wisconsin. As with many in that north-central region of the United States, he has a mixed cultural heritage that can be traced back to Norway, Slovakia, Ireland and the Netherlands. That he has spent much of his adult life affiliated to Nordic organizations and living in Scandinavia speaks to his personal sense of adventure but can also be read as a homecoming of sorts, a return to his roots. Fluent in Danish, with a high level of competence in other Scandinavian languages, Chris nevertheless remains an Anglophone and will forever be an outsider in the country that he now calls home. Yet it is a status that he cherishes, his personal transatlantic bridging provides a purpose to the work he carries out with Henrik, helping companies internationalize their businesses from both a commercial and cultural standpoint. Chris belongs and does not belong, and this supplies him with singular insights about how Nordic leadership works and its relevance beyond the region itself.

As a young man, a short period of study in Aalborg—his first taste of life in the Nordics—was followed by more extensive travels through Europe, exercising a wanderlust he had first experienced hitch-hiking across the United States. He returned to his homeland where he completed a degree in International Relations at the University of Minnesota. Chris then embarked upon a professional relationship that would endure for more than two decades, entering the Scandinavian Airlines (SAS) Management Trainee Program. His career with the airline took him from Seattle to New York to the head office in Stockholm to Copenhagen and, finally, to Milan. Denmark exercised the strongest hold, the home of his children, and it was to Copenhagen that he returned and reinvented himself once he took the decision to part ways with SAS.

While still at SAS, Chris studied for an MBA at the Henley Business School in Denmark. It established a new connection with executive education that resulted in Chris joining the board of International Management Education (IME), deepening his interest in Nordic leadership and its practice in different contexts.

Eventually, in 2016, Chris assumed a dual managing director role with oversight of both IME and Henley Business School in Denmark.

Henrik was born into a middle-class family in Copenhagen. Life was comfortable and school was easy, which led Henrik to seek knowledge and experiences elsewhere. From a young age, he demonstrated entrepreneurial prowess, with various small business initiatives to make money funding his fascination with technology and the acquisition of the latest gadgets. Surrounded by smart people at high school and university, however, Henrik learned how to stretch himself academically too, realizing the benefits of effort and application.

Lifelong learning characterizes Henrik's approach to study, paid endeavor and play. This is evident in the variety of ventures he has been involved in, his work in the public, private and start-up sectors, as well as his formal education. Over the years, he has gone on to acquire a Master's degree in Electrical Engineering from the Technical University of Denmark and another business-oriented degree from the Copenhagen Business School. He also has spent time studying at the CIO Academy in Oxford, at the INSEAD campuses in both Singapore and France, and at Stanford University, where he focused on entrepreneurship. His engineering background and interest in computer science have provided firm foundations—administrative and leadership experiences adding further strings to his bow. Even during the period of his Master's degree, Henrik was providing consultancy services via his own business and picking up other work as an audio-visual technician at high-profile conferences.

Following graduation, the natural choice for Henrik as a long-term career was that of a chief information officer. At the time, this was a relatively new kind of executive role reflecting the increasing importance of digital technologies in business and government. His chosen career path has led to Henrik working for prominent organizations, including Carlsberg, Gartner, Navision and the Danish Ministry of Finance. This has taken him from Denmark to Southeast Asia to Australia to France to California, where he now works with Chris at Advant Partners and has a role with Hampleton Partners where he advises on mergers and acquisitions. He and his family have settled on a vineyard, establishing their own label, Odin Wine, which acknowledges their Norse heritage. Today, Henrik straddles the boundary between big business and the start-up community. He draws on his personal experience regarding the application of Nordic leadership and its modification for different cultures and business contexts.

In researching this book and reflecting on our own stories, we have enriched our understanding of the subject through extensive interviews and conversations with a host of theorists and practitioners across a range of industries and disciplines. These include politicians, academics, entrepreneurs, business executives, consultants, philosophers, economists, environmental activists, sports people, lawyers and historians. They come from many walks of life, from different social, cultural and geographical backgrounds. Yet together they offer great understanding of and insight into Nordic leadership.

The Nordics include the Scandinavian nations of Denmark, Norway and Sweden, their neighbor Finland, the island-nation Iceland, the autonomous territories of the Faroe Islands, Greenland and Åland, and the Sámi regions that extend eastwards into Russia. Many of the interviewees for this book hail from the Nordic area. But not all. Several are part of other cultures and have a connection to the Nordics through family, study or work. Their perspective brings another dimension to the insider–outsider approach that Chris and Henrik applied to their research. So too the nuances unveiled by several people who have lived and worked in more than one Nordic nation or territory.

Chris likes both to encourage and tease friends and colleagues in the Nordics. It is not hard to understand why. "This is your time," he tells them. "The world is looking at you." Without doubt, there is a Nordic zeitgeist that is drawing others in as the story continues to unfold. By way of example, in the lead up to Christmas 2016, any visitor to a British bookstore would have found it difficult to avoid the tables overburdened with hefty tomes dedicated to such topics as *hygge* (the conceptualization of cozy), *fika* (a small communal meal), Nordic cuisine and wood-cutting techniques. 2017 held out the promise of yet more Nordic lifestyle books, dedicated to the Swedish concept of *lagom* (just the right amount) and the Norwegian and Danish notion of *friluftsliv* (outdoor living). This latest wave of enthusiasm in the United Kingdom for customs Northern follows close on the heels of a global fascination with the literary, cinematic and televisual manifestations of Nordic Noir. The small screen has been filled with season after season of subtitled explorations of the darker side of humanity, presented in muted tones and varying degrees of existential angst—or with remakes of the same in English, French and Spanish, adapted for local markets.

Yet the artistic and cultural interest in the Nordics represents but the tip of the iceberg. The Nordics have been attracting attention for any number of political, societal, design, environmental, educational and economic reasons. For example, numerous mentions of Denmark were made by candidates during the 2016 US presidential elections. In his 2011 book *The Origins of Political Order*, political economist Francis Fukuyama identifies "Getting to Denmark" as the ideal goal for establishing societies that are creative, peaceful, inclusive and prosperous.

According to regular studies and surveys, the Nordic nations are among the happiest places to live—although one interviewee for this book mischievously suggests that this is because people in these countries have low expectations; after half a year in the darkness of an extended winter, just seeing some sun, feeling its warmth on your skin, is enough to bring a smile to the face. Then again, a willingness not to take oneself too seriously could be another source of happiness. So too being surrounded by the natural beauty of the mountains, forests, fjords and polar ice caps, or the elegant urban design of Nordic cityscapes, friendlier to the pedestrian and cyclist than the car driver. But this acknowledgment of happiness is offset to some extent by the melancholia that is a characteristic of many aspects of Nordic culture. This is evidenced, for example, by the philosophy of Søren Kierkegaard, the paintings of Edvard Munch, the theatre of August Strindberg and Henrik Ibsen, the cinema of Ingmar Bergman or the music of Jean Sibelius.

There are any number of other spheres where the Nordics feature prominently, serving as a source of inspiration for others. Many of the Nordic nations practice an innovative and successful approach to learning, not only for the school-aged but for infants and adults too, from the forest pre-schools to N. F. S. Grundtvig's folk high schools to the universities and business schools. Finland, in particular, attracts much attention today for its ideas about mainstream education and its relevance to later life. The region also is at the forefront of the development and harnessing of sustainable energy sources. Norway may have rich oil reserves, but other Nordic nations have exploited both hydro and wind power, their initial forays in these fields now widely imitated by other countries.

The Nordics also are admired for the advances they have made in equality and human rights, leading the way, for example, with freedom of information, free speech, same-sex marriage and women's emancipation. In Lars Rebien Sørensen, they have a figure who has been recognized as the best chief executive in the world during his tenure at Novo Nordisk. In Noma, an establishment frequently acknowledged as the best restaurant in the world, forever pushing at the boundaries. In the Lego Group, the world's most powerful brand. In Iceland's Vigdís Finnbogadóttir, the first woman to be democratically elected president of a state. In Carl Theodor Dreyer, Ingmar Bergman and Lars von Trier, figures who changed the language of cinema. The same can be said in the fields of architecture, design, software, medicine, biotech, quantum physics, fertility treatment, classical music, painting, theatre and literature. The Nordics are often to be found at the vanguard of creativity and innovation. One quantifiable measure is the fact that although the Nordics account for only 8% of European GDP, the Northern countries account for 50% of the European start-ups that exceed the $1bn valuation, achieving "unicorn" status. On a global scale, the Nordics account for 2% of global GDP, but produced 7% of the 2016 exits valued above $1bn.

We live in times of extreme uncertainty, yet the Nordic nations seemingly have found a way to navigate through them. They have managed so far to combine free-market capitalism and a well-structured welfare state, to balance purpose with sustainable profit, enabling a strong sense of community and respect for the environment, and instilling a collaborative approach that scales from the individual to the societal level, founded as it is upon trust-based relationships. Their societies promote the autonomy of the individual in service of the collective. The collaborative emphasis in their project-based school work contrasts sharply with the promotion of competition that characterizes many other cultures, which rely on quantification, assessment and league tables. Collaboration and cooperation are effective in the workplace and in coalition politics in the Nordics because they come naturally. This way of thinking and acting is what people have known all their lives.

In May 2016, during his last year in office, US President Barack Obama hosted the leaders of the five Nordic nations at a state dinner in the White House. The President's toast to his guests was one of cultural collage, acknowledging their Viking heritage, folk school tradition and leadership on matters relating to equality and climate change. Obama concluded by recognizing their global role. "I've said it before and I will repeat, they punch above their weight. In their values, in their contributions, not just to making their own countries function well, but to make the whole world a better place makes them one of our most valuable partners everywhere in the world." David stands shoulder-to-shoulder with Goliath.

The economist E. F. Schumacher argued that small is beautiful. In this sense, the Nordics achieve a confederacy of beauty, stronger than the sum of their parts, like the Icelandic soccer team. Individually each of the nations is small but collectively they represent one of the larger global economies and exercise a disproportionate influence on world matters. Politician, activist and poet Birgitta Jónsdóttir indicates that with small nations it is easier to quickly reach critical mass, enabling change, getting things done. The flip side, of course, as witnessed in Iceland's recent history, is that small communities can become breeding grounds for nepotism. Checks and balances are required to ensure that the faith placed in leadership and in the state are not abused. Individuals cannot abdicate their responsibility to the institution while still retaining a sense of entitlement.

Today, the Nordics have found strength in numbers, united by similarities, benefiting from nuanced differences, whether of language or landscape or practice. They will joke about one another's leadership competencies, the Finns' speed to action, the Swedes' paralysis by consensus, but it is a familial, friendly kind of teasing. Together they form the Nordic Council, individually they participate in international communities. All are members of the United Nations; Denmark, Finland and Sweden of the European Union; and Denmark, Iceland and Norway of NATO. Historically, however, the region has endured periods of volatility, invasions, shared monarchies and independence struggles. From the middle of the nineteenth century, shadows have been cast by larger, militarily-potent neighbors: Germany to the south, Russia to the east and the United States to the west. As with their Viking forebears, whose reach extended to all points of the compass, the modern Nordics have found a way to be connectors. For example, it was Iceland that facilitated the 1986 Cold War summit between Reagan and Gorbachev. More recently, it is the burgeoning Nordic tech sector that is seeking alliances in an emergent Chinese market. The Nordic outlook is global rather than insular, commanding respect on the world stage.

Trust lies behind the perception of Nordic success. It has been a recurrent theme in every interview conducted for this book. Trust is the glue of Nordic societies, implicit in interactions between people at one level and between the member states of the Nordic Council at another. It is commonplace for citizens to trust institutions and government; the payment of high taxes, for example, understood as a signifier of the faith vested in the welfare state. As the telephone conversation that Henrik over-heard suggests, it is usual for leaders to trust the judgment and action of their colleagues, and for team members to feel confi-dent that they share a common purpose with their bosses. In global terms, incidences of political or corporate corruption in the Nordic nations are rare, the recent Icelandic examples are anomalies that prove the rule. When they are unearthed, a sense of betrayal manifests itself at a societal level. A breach of client or citizen trust, on occasion, can be dealt with far more harshly than other forms of criminal offence such as theft or even mur-der. In the latter, the victims are few in number, in the former, a multitude is affected and the system requires rebalancing due to the breach of the very fabric that these nations are built on.

For both Italian lawyer Massimo Caiazza and Finnish entrepre-neur Mika Anttonen, the assumption of trust in a Nordic context has an accelerating effect corporately, societally and politically. Trust-based relationships quickly move things forward in busi-ness meetings, between companies, between Nordic nations, and in an individual's relationship with the state. There is less of a need for preamble, for getting to know one another, for weighing other people up and gaining understanding of them. Meetings, even when there is an underlying desire for consen-sus, can move rapidly to the discussion of detail necessary to make decisions. Such blind faith in other people and their good will, however, is not without its pitfalls.

In the late 1990s, a couple in Brooklyn had their child removed from them and temporarily put into foster care. The offence for which the Danish mother and US-based father were arrested and charged was neglect. Their crime? Leaving their daughter in a stroller on the street while dining in a restaurant. What is commonplace in Denmark, founded on the expectation that other people will do the right thing, proved to be a criminal offence in the United States where the default is distrust of others in a competitive society. The story neatly demonstrates the strength of trust in Nordic societies while also highlighting what some perceive as a shortcoming. Namely that an over-reliance on trust is a sign of naivety, that it leaves the individual, the organization or community vulnerable to exploitation. This is a perspective that several non-nationals—such as Mel McCall of the United Kingdom and Carmen Sanz of Spain—who have spent time either living in the Nordics or working overseas with Nordic companies, were quick to share with Chris and Henrik.

Massimo has gained admission to the bar in both his native Italy and in Sweden. His life is multicultural, not only requiring linguistic fluency in Italian, Swedish and English, but necessitating a deep understanding of social norms in the different nations. He has admired the effects of a Swedish education on his own children, yet he has had to work hard to overcome his own social conditioning in Italian society. In a telling insight, Massimo comments that in Italy the only people who are trusted are members of your own family. Distrust of the institution, of the state, of outsiders, is a given. There is a tendency towards secrecy and closure rather than the openness and trust that characterize Nordic societies. A similar observation was made by Mika regarding what he has witnessed during time spent in Greece, especially in the wake of the financial crisis that has impacted the country in recent years. Authority and institutions are treated with deep suspicion, security is sought in the family.

Ally Jiang is Chinese. She has worked in the fields of learning and development and talent management at the Carlsberg Group both in China and Denmark. More recently, Ally has

joined Saxo Bank, based in Copenhagen. One of the most striking things she has noticed about working in Danish companies
is that, on entering a room, it is far more difficult to identify who
the leader is than in a Chinese organization. In a Danish company, there is less overt hierarchy, less focus on quantification,
less command-and-control, than Ally encountered under Chinese management and leadership. During her time in Denmark,
Ally has found that greater emphasis is placed on people, their
participation and the realization of their potential than in China. Carmen echoes these sentiments in a different international
context, distinguishing between Spanish business culture and
her experiences representing Norwegian organizations via the
chamber of commerce she runs in the Madrid area.

The democratic impulse, the need for consensus, can at first be
unnerving for outsiders more used to an authoritarian style of
leadership. Certainly, Chris struggled with the requirement to
express a view when he first started working in Sweden. He was
not simply being told what to do but was expected to participate
in the decision-making process. He needed to have an opinion
and show willingness in sharing it. At some point, though, discussion stops and the leader decides, talk transitioning into action, with ownership and accountability clear for all.

Like Chris, Annelise Goldstein, a human resources executive,
has a hybridized US–Danish outlook. She has a parent from
each country and has spent time living in both. Her formative
years, though, were spent in the United States, so returning to
Denmark has required adaptation, not just linguistically but behaviorally too. Annelise, like many interviewees, comments on
the low power distance evident in many Nordic companies. This
manifests itself not only in their flatter organizational structures but also in the more equitable, closer pay ratio between

the highest and lowest earners. The egalitarianism and wealth distribution of Nordic societies is neatly captured in a passage from Peter Høeg's novel *Frøken Smillas fornemmelse for sne* (*Smilla's Sense of Snow*). "Seen from my perspective, Denmark's entire population is middle-class. The truly poor and the truly rich are so few as to be almost exotic." Annelise also appreciates the accessibility of senior Nordic leaders. During her time at Novo Nordisk, for example, she valued how leaders were available to talk to, how they listened, how they sought out the opinions of other people.

Annelise has found colleagues that she has worked with in Denmark to be open, honest and humble; characteristics that are fundamental to building trust-based relationships. Marco Sammicheli is an Italian journalist, curator and academic who has married into a Danish family. He too values the openness and trust that he associates with Nordic societies. But he highlights another aspect that stands in contrast to what he knows in his native country: namely, the reliability, correctness and pragmatism with which Nordic people do things. Jo Ashman, a UK-based former member of the Scandinavian Airlines team, associates such traits with the Nordic pursuit of quality. For Jo, this is evident in their service industries, in their products and in their athletes, from soccer and tennis players to golfers and skiers. He observes that the quality of a Nordic product tends to justify the fact that it is rarely cheap. Form meets function; aesthetics and design in perfect harmony.

The Hofstede cultural dimensions theory is the brainchild of Dutch social psychologist Geert Hofstede. It establishes connections between a society's culture, the values upheld by its people and the behaviors such values foster. In examining national cultures, the Hofstede theory takes into account a range of indices that make it possible to identify generalized differences between nations. These cover power distance, individualism versus collectivism, masculinity versus femininity, uncertainty avoidance, long-term versus short-term orientation, and indulgence versus restraint. On each of these indices, there are more similarities than differences between the Nordic nations. For example, they all evidence a feminine orientation, suggesting an aptitude for cooperation, a self-effacing tendency towards modesty and humility, and a desire to care for others that is visible in their welfare states. Given the high placement of these countries in international studies of happiness, it is also no surprise to find all five Nordic nations recognized as indulgent, even if Finland and Norway score more modestly than the other three.

Low	Power distance	High
Collectivist	Collectivism/Indivdualism	Individualistic
Low	Uncertainty avoidance	High
Feminine	Feminine/Masculine	Masculine
Long term	Long term/short term orientation	Short term
Restraint	Restraint/Indulgence	Indulgence

Gert Hofstede's Dimensions of Culture

In Hofstede's study, the Nordics are portrayed as individualist societies in which *I* outweighs *we*. This may be the case in terms of indulgence but, as the feminine orientation of each country suggests, there still remains a strong interest in the collective. As psychologist Angela Duckworth frames it in her book *Grit,* "each of us enriches the environment of all of us". In some respects, *hygge* and *fika* have become signifiers of indulgence and comfort. Yet even these examples are not completely self-serving as they are as often about connection, about creating perfect moments for others, as they are about doing so for oneself. Indeed, economist, philosopher and futurist Lene Rachel Andersen has researched the manner in which interests scale from the well-being of the individual to the family to the community to the nation to the Nordic region itself. The further from the individual you get, the less a concept like *hygge* applies. Yet that individual still remains personally invested in these different domains to varying degrees.

A Nordic tax payer, for example, relinquishes a large proportion of their income for the common good. A Nordic employee enjoys a high degree of autonomy but they do so in service of shared objectives. Each person has a voice and democratic rights. They question and challenge in order to understand, to gain and share knowledge, enabling better decision-making. They do not simply follow the herd. It is in this sense, rather than through selfishness, that individualism prevails in Nordic nations. Autonomy within loose frameworks, improving the wealth and well-being of the community. These are egalitarian, inclusive, participative societies that welcome and value the efforts of the individual. In their communities—as a collective of people, in their coalition politics, in their international alliances—they demonstrate how their collective strength is greater than the sum of their parts.

Mirroring Annelise's personal experience, Denmark leads the way in terms of its low power distance and its breakdown of traditional hierarchical authority. Its Hofstede index score of 18 contrasts sharply with the score of 40 for the United States and 93 for Russia. Denmark and Sweden are also at the vanguard in terms of their willingness to embrace uncertainty, their adaptiveness essential to navigating the complexities of the modern world. This cannot be attributed simply to environmental conditioning, as their neighbors' scores suggest a higher degree of risk aversion, while influential world powers like Germany and particularly Russia demonstrate much greater intolerance of uncertainty. Collectively, the Nordics lean towards tradition and a suspicion of change, yet when change happens they demonstrate responsiveness to it, even responsibility for it.

These are societies in which the entrepreneurial start-up—the disruptor of established industries, an agitator for change—sits comfortably alongside the infrastructure of the welfare state. Cultures in which the historical legacy of the Viking age is celebrated alongside the civil liberties of the modern era. The welfare state, in fact, mitigates risks taken on by the entrepreneur; there is a safety net in case of failure. But for every Skype, Spotify or Supercell founded in the Nordic region there is also an established corporate giant like Maersk, IKEA or Statoil. What is fascinating about these organizations, big and small, is that the fundamentals of Nordic leadership tend to prevail even as the companies grow. This contrasts with what is documented elsewhere. In Silicon Valley, for example, many characteristics associated with Nordic leadership are evident in the start-up community. But as these companies mature and grow, there is a tendency to adapt operating models. Venture capitalists parachute in experienced corporate leaders, new layers of management are added, and what was once flat becomes pyramidal in structure. This raises questions about the exportability of Nordic leadership, which will remain a motif throughout this book.

The Social Progress Index explores different dimensions to Hofstede. It aggregates social and environmental data from 128 countries to assess how nations perform in relation to meeting basic human needs, such as nutrition, access to water, sanitation, shelter and personal safety; establishing the foundations of wellbeing, including literacy, education, access to information, life expectancy and environmental quality; and providing opportunities for people, which embraces factors like freedom of expression, political rights, inclusion, equality and levels of corruption. Yet again, the Nordics perform extraordinarily strongly in a global context. In the June 2017 findings, Denmark was positioned first, Finland second, Iceland and Norway joint third, and Sweden eighth. Only the performance of progressive nations like Switzerland, Canada and the Netherlands prevented a Nordic clean sweep of all the top positions.

Rank	Country	Score
1	Denmark	90.57
2	Finland	90.53
3	Iceland	90.27
3	Norway	90.27
5	Switzerland	90.10
6	Canada	89.84
7	Netherlands	89.82
8	Sweden	89.66
9	Australia	89.30
9	New Zealand	89.30
11	Ireland	88.91
12	United Kingdom	88.73
13	Germany	88.50
14	Austria	87.98

Ranking of very high social progess (Social Progress Imperative, 2017)

That there is something that we can label *Nordic Leadership*, whether applied socio-politically or corporately, is becoming increasingly evident. It is attracting the interest of politicians and business people keen on marketing the Nordic region, in addition to that of academics and theorists, researchers and

Basic Human Needs	Foundations of Wellbeing	Opportunity
Nutrition and Basic Medical Care	**Access to Basic Knowledge**	**Personal Rights**
Undernourishment	Adult literacy rate	Political rights
Depth of food deficit	Primary school	Freedom of expression
Maternal mortality rate	enrollment	Freedom of assembly
Child mortality rate	Secondary school	Private property rights
Deaths from infectious	enrollment	
diseases	Gender parity in	**Personal Freedom**
	secondary enrollment	**and Choice**
Water and Sanitation		Freedom over life choices
Access to piped water	**Access to Information**	Freedom of religion
Rural access to improved	**and Communications**	Early marriage
water source	Mobile telephone	Satisfied demand for
Access to improved sani-	subscriptions	contraception
tation facilities	Internet users	Corruption
	Press Freedom Index	
Shelter		**Tolerance and Inclusion**
Availability of affordable		Tolerance for immigrants
housing	**Health and Wellness**	Tolerance for
Access to electricity	Life expectancy at 60	homosexuals
Quality of electricity	Premature deaths from	Discrimination and
supply	non-communicable	violence against
Household air pollution	diseases	minorities
attributable deaths?	Suicide rate	Religious tolerance
		Community safety net
Personal Safety	**Environmental Quality**	
Homicide rate	Outdoor air pollution	**Access to Advanced**
Level of violent crime	attributable deaths	**Education**
Perceived criminality	Wastewater treatment	Years of tertiary
Political terror	Biodiversity and habitat	schooling
Traffic deaths	Greenhouse gas	Women's average years
	emissions	in school
		Inequality in the
		attainment of education
		Globally ranked
		universities
		Percentage of tertiary
		studens enrolled in
		globally ranked
		universities

Social Progress Index indicator-level frame work (Social Progress Index, 2017)

practitioners. A steady stream of published work is raising the visibility and furthering the understanding of what this means. These include *The Viking Manifesto* (2007) by Steve Strid and Claes Andréasson, *Nordic Lights* (2007) by Henrik Holt Larsen and Ulla Bruun de Neergaard, *Viking Economics* (2016) by George Lakey, *The Nordic Theory of Everything* (2016) by Anu Partanen, and *Nordic Ways* (2016), an essay collection written by an array of public figures from the Nordic region, overseen by András Simonyi and edited by Debra Cagan. Further publications are imminent, including *The Nordic Secret* by Lene Rachel Andersen and Tomas Björkman, as well as Tor Grønsund's *Startup Vikings*. Jón Baldvin Hannibalsson, an Icelandic politician and diplomat, when interviewed for this book, informed the authors that today he spends a significant proportion of his time teaching Nordic leadership ideas to students in the Baltic States. Meanwhile, Chris is overseeing courses on the topic delivered to a global business community by IME.

If President Obama's 2016 speech further helped bring Nordic appreciation into focus, then Rufus Gifford, the US ambassador to Denmark until the new President, Donald Trump, assumed office in January 2017, wonders whether the Nordic peoples will go ahead and "own the zeitgeist". Having established a successful formula, nurtured a specific culture, in their own nations, can they help this vision be realized elsewhere? Indeed, to sustain the success of the Nordic model, is it in fact necessary to practice in new territories, in the Americas, in Asia, in Africa? Do the advocates of Nordic leadership need to follow their Viking forebears in traveling to new lands, exploring and discovering, in order to sustain, adapt and progress the way of life they value so dearly? Or do new challenges at home open up further opportunities there too? Rufus is witness to both approaches through his board work with Danish organizations.

Per Tryding, of the Chamber of Commerce and Industry of Southern Sweden, detects a certain shift in those Nordic organizations that have a multinational presence. In the past, they exported their leaders, installing them in foreign lands to work with an indigenous workforce. Now it tends to be the ideas that are exported and leadership potential is identified and nurtured locally. Cultures and styles are blended. It is a collaborative rather than imperial approach. Vincent Hendricks, Professor of Formal Philosophy and Director of the Center for Information and Bubble Studies (CIBS) at University of Copenhagen, speaks of the homogeneity of Nordic societies. This may have been their source of strength in the past, establishing communal bonds, enabling shared beliefs and common values, from the Norse mythology of a Viking past through Lutheran doctrine and on to modern secularism. But that homogeneity is gradually undergoing change, affected by open markets, international alliances and immigration.

Vincent himself is both an African-American and a Dane. He describes himself as "a New Yorker misplaced in Copenhagen", living bi-culturally. It is a sentiment echoed by Henrik, as a Dane who has settled in US but has become closely involved in an expatriate community while there, serving as the president of the Danish–American Chamber of Commerce in California. Another interviewee, Humphrey Lau, is Danish-Chinese. He moved with his family to Denmark when very young, grew up in that country and now works in China. These are people who are simultaneously Nordic and global citizens, who live and work in multiple places. They have to adapt to wherever they find themselves, even if they carry with them a cultural heritage rooted in Danish society, values and education. In Walt Whitman's words, they "contain multitudes".

The assimilation of economic migrants and refugees from war zones is also gradually adding to the diversity of Nordic society, presenting new challenges and new opportunities going forward. Yet history suggests that assimilation and adaptation has always been the Nordic way. At home and abroad, evidenced by the Viking settlements in places like England, Scotland, Ireland and France, their voyages to more distant locations to the east, the south and the west, and their accumulation of knowledge, people and artifacts from these foreign lands. Actions overseas have always found their way back home in some form; the practices of the Nordics exported, those of other lands imported, in a constant cultural exchange. Did the influence of the Irish writing tradition, for example, assimilated either from thralls or from earlier settlers, contribute to the codification of Viking culture on Iceland? It is to those Viking antecedents and their legacy that we now briefly turn.

CHAPTER 2
VIKING

No better burden a man bears on the road
than a store of common sense;
better than riches it will seem in an unfamiliar place,
such is the resort of the wretched.
~ *The Poetic Edda*, Sayings of the High One, Stanza 10

It is, though, in the power of their words and deeds
to stir the imagination that the Vikings have left their
most potent legacy. For a people addicted to sagas, and
for whom there was nothing more important than that
their reputation lived on in the memory of those who
witnessed their deeds, this is perhaps the most fitting
memorial of all.
~ Philip Parker, *The Northmen's Fury*

In J. R. R. Tolkien's *Lord of the Rings* cycle, characters are often
introduced in terms of their paternal lineage. Who was their

father? Who was their grandfather? What is their ancestral bloodline? Tolkien was influenced by ancient Norse texts, skaldic poetry and the Icelandic sagas, which continue to exercise an influence both within and outside the Nordic region, as witness Neil Gaiman's 2017 publication of *Norse Mythology*. Runes, the *Edda* and the sagas are all time capsules, purveyors of Viking culture that we are still able to access today. The role of family and community was central to this culture, providing a sense of belonging. To be descended from a good family, whether a mortal human, a god or a giant, commanded respect and assigned status to the individual, reinforced by their personal actions and behaviors.

Viking families were located in small communities, which themselves centered on agricultural, maritime and craft activities. Within those communities there were strong interdependencies, founded upon trust-based relationships. This was essential to survival. Fish had to be caught, crops planted and harvested, wood cut, buildings constructed, to nurture the community and protect it from the harshness of winter. Weapons had to be made, sea vessels too, either for transporting people or cargo. Leaders emerged from within these communities, first among equals, commanding respect and distributing wealth.

These two forms of capital, social and financial, were serviced by forays either overseas or into the territory of other Viking communities. Raids enabled Viking leaders to demonstrate their own bravery in battle, thereby earning recognition from their comrades, and to accumulate spoils that could be shared with the community back home. Such raids required an initial investment in the construction of a ship, and the support of local people who would crew it. According to Morten Ravn, archaeologist and curator at the Viking Ship Museum in Roskilde, a crew on board a large longship would number around 60 people. This would be both a maritime and fighting unit, equipped for amphibian warfare. The size of the Viking war fleets varied greatly. Some consisted of a handful of ships, while others consisted of several hundred. No matter the size, however, the self-commanding military units, comprised of a longship's crew, were the backbone of the military operations.

Among an amphibian unit, there would be specialist warriors allied to the leaders, as well as generalists from the community, part-sailors, part-warriors, part-farmers or craftsmen. Morten believes that the proximity of these individuals in the confined space of a Viking ship, the trust that they had to place in one another to fulfill their roles, especially when rowing, alongside the weapons training they would have undergone together, allowed these groups to cohere into tight-knit units in a relatively short space of time. As sailors, as warriors, the crew had to look out for one another, encourage each other and demonstrate bravery in stressful conditions, whether at sea or in battle. Life on board a ship would have been like a boot camp for the raids and conflicts they sailed towards. These common experiences established bonds for life.

The relatively small size of the Viking units also made them extremely adaptive. So too the fact that their vessels could be maneuvered by either sail or oar, thereby removing the dependency on favorable winds to make their escape after rapid insurgent action. This was a unique combination on the northern seas. The Viking ships' draft of less than a meter allowed for them to be sailed not only on the open sea but in shallow waters, even up rivers. The flatter bottoms also made it possible to land on beaches, not unlike the actions of the Allies in Normandy during World War II. The Viking crews not only were fierce warriors but highly skilled sailors and oarsmen. Records made by those who witnessed the aftermath of Viking raids on places like Lindisfarne speak of them appearing from nowhere and departing before any defense could be mounted.

The organization of the crews on board ship has been an area of specialist research for Morten. In 2016, he published his study *Viking Age War Fleets*. He has drawn on diverse sources, including archeological finds, written records and images to inform his understanding of roles, leadership, communication and navigation on a Viking ship. When sailing or paddling, it is usual to face the direction of travel. When rowing, however, the oarsmen have their backs to the ship's bow. In other words, trust and confidence had to be placed in the captain, the helmsman and their lookouts who would be the only ones facing forward. Communication would already have been difficult aboard the long, narrow ships, given the noise of wind and waves. It was further complicated when the sail was raised. The latter also impaired visibility for the captain or helmsman who would be located in the stern of the ship.

Morten argues that sections of the Bayeux Tapestry, which show William the Conqueror's fleet on the English Channel, explain how the Vikings overcame such limitations and learned to deal with the complexities presented by maritime navigation. These show a middleman positioned by the mast relaying messages back and forth between lookouts and helmsman. The Normans were themselves descended from Norsemen settlers and continued many traditions associated with the Scandinavian lands from which their Viking ancestors had come. In effect, King Harold Godwinson defeated one Viking army, under the leadership of Harald Hardrada of Norway, at Stamford Bridge in September 1066, only to succumb to another one at the Battle of Hastings nineteen days later. The Danelaw metamorphosed into the Norman occupation of England.

The Viking pattern of raids was one way of securing communal wealth and personal recognition. But this inevitably led to settlement and occupancy too. Curiosity and seafaring capabilities resulted in exploration, navigation of unmapped lands, the establishment of new trade routes and unexpected alliances. In March 2017, *National Geographic* reflected the resurgence of enthusiasm for Viking history and legacy among the territories with which they came into contact. This has seen numerous television documentary and drama productions over recent years, as well as battle re-enactments and high-profile Viking and longship exhibitions, including a 2017 virtual reality installation at the Yorkshire Museum. The image of a Viking warrior was featured on the front cover of the magazine, which included an extensive article on Viking culture. The National Geographic article, by science writer Heather Pringle, drew on the work of Morten and other Viking specialists, including archeological research, as well as discoveries made using modern technologies such as satellite imagery, DNA studies and isotope analysis. It manages to convey the incredible diaspora the Vikings achieved.

Large swathes of England, Ireland, Wales, mainland Scotland and the islands to the north and west of it were either settled by Vikings or used as base camps as they advanced to destinations further afield. The Shetland Islands, for example, were on the route to Scotland and Ireland for the Norwegian Vikings, while the Faroe Islands were found roughly at the mid-point of voyages from Bergen to Reykjavík. York and the surrounding region was a short journey from Denmark, and Anglo-Saxon lands further south in East Anglia and Kent could be reached with ease. Iceland itself led to Greenland, where settlements were established on the western coast. From there, the sagas and more recent archeological finds tell us that the Vikings travelled to Newfoundland, Vinland and possibly beyond into the North American continent several centuries before Columbus found himself on land in the Caribbean.

The entire northern coastline of mainland Europe was subject to extensive Viking raids over the centuries. These affected modern-day Germany, the Netherlands, Belgium and France. The numerous raids along rivers reached far inland in France, posing a threat to Paris. Frequent besiegements often resulted in *Danegeld* ransom payments made by the Franks during the ninth and tenth centuries. It was through vassalage and negotiation, though, that the Vikings were able to secure and settle Normandy under Rollo's leadership. They appeared further south too, with raids recorded in Poitiers, Bordeaux and Toulouse, in the Spanish regions of Galicia, Andalusia, Catalonia and the Balearic Islands, in Portugal and on the southern French coast, as well as in northwestern Italy.

To the north, the Vikings explored areas of the Arctic Circle, venturing into the Sámi territory of the White Sea. To the east, they settled part of Poland. Their navigation skills, along the Gulf of Finland and through the river networks to the south, also resulted in the settlement of parts of modern Russia, Belarus and the Ukraine. They were even known to have fought battles and conducted raids on the Caspian Sea. Their traversing of the Black Sea brought them to Constantinople, where Byzantine emperors recruited Norse mercenaries into the Varangian Guard, an elite unit of the Byzantine Army. On their travels, the Vikings established contact with over fifty different cultures. Land settlement and prowess in battle earned recognition from European monarchs, emperors and popes willing to engage in diplomatic relations with them.

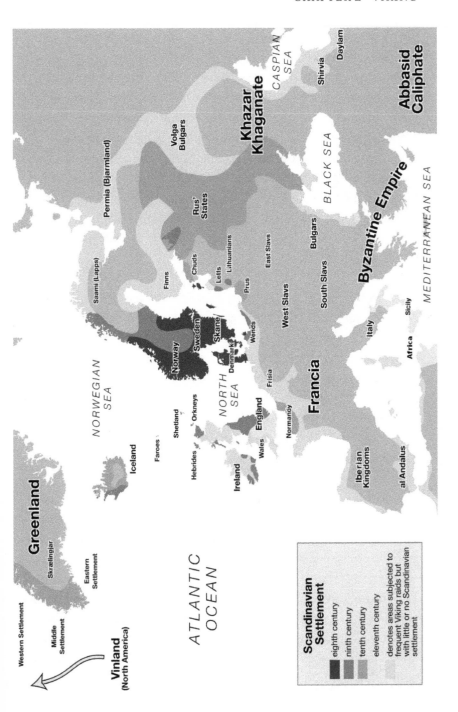

Viking expansion. Map by Max Naylor (Wikipedia Commons)

The Vikings' own territories were in effect a network of communities clustered in the Nordic countries, Britain, Ireland, Normandy and the Rus area. These were characterized by fluid strategic alliances between different chieftains. Norse monarchs were installed who were entirely dependent on their relationships with these chieftains and magnates, their power a reflection of the union of communities. In this sense, kingdoms were less spatial entities, more relational ones, with borders shifting in accordance with different friendships and partnerships. There was no singular, holistic Viking realm or empire. Rather a patchwork of loosely connected territories, linked by wanderlust and seafaring capability.

The developmental psychologist Erik Erikson, the social psychologist Mihalyi Csikszentmihalyi and the evolutionary biologist Mark Pagel all make the case that humans serve two distinct but interrelated purposes: the perpetuation of the species through procreation and the dissemination of our culture. In Csikszentmihalyi's phrase, we possess an innate ability, especially in our middle years, to pass on our genes and our memes. This the Vikings achieved to an extraordinary extent in the medieval period of human civilization. Their DNA was spread from Uzbekistan to Canada, while traces of their language can still be found not only in Icelandic and the different Scandinavian tongues, but in the regional dialects of northern England and Scotland too. In the Cumbrian region, for example, topographical terms like *dale, pike, fell, scar, howe, beck* and *tarn* all have Norse origins.

The Vikings found other ways to stay present in our modern world. Viking ship burials and rune stones shape parts of the landscape in their former lands. Their rune graffiti can also be found in the places they visited such as the Hagia Sophia in Istanbul. Meanwhile, Norse mythology endures, still read in the original and in translation, inspiring the work of modern writers, graphic novelists and filmmakers. Even in those nations that enjoy parliamentary democracies, we find echoes of the Viking's Icelandic Althing, Faroese Løgting and Manx Tynwald. Their influence endures in far-reaching ways that many do not appreciate, having no conception of their roots. Even in the modern era, as with their Viking forebears, Nordics who make their name overseas and return with reputations enhanced or spoils to share are celebrated. This applies as much to the celebrated sports personality, musician, chef or business entrepreneur as it does to the polar explorer Roald Amundsen and *Kon-Tiki* adventurer Thor Heyerdahl.

Yet a cultural stereotype prevails that made many of the people interviewed for this book uneasy about their Viking heritage. They were quick to caveat, to distance, to contrast a peaceful present with a bellicose past. Morten was an exception, steeped as he is in an appreciation of Viking history and able to draw parallels between what happened in the past and in contemporary Nordic societies. However, few others demonstrated pride in their Viking ancestry. For many, their associations were distasteful, linked to notions of rape and pillage, terrorism, slavery and dislocation. Some expressed surprise that people in areas associated with devastating acts of destruction or brutality now whitewashed their past, marketing their connections to the Vikings, establishing a tourist industry around them. Jón Baldvin Hannibalsson recounts an experience when Icelandic Minister of Finance. He was visiting his Irish counterpart and was introduced to their grandsons. When the Irish Finance Minister explained that a real-life Viking stood before them, the boys fled the room and hid themselves. The tainted Viking reputation had preceded Jón, the stereotype usurping the flesh-and-blood reality.

A more considered appreciation of the period reveals that, while fierce fighters, with the Berserkers earning particular renown, the Vikings were simply a reflection of the era in which they lived. They certainly were not the only people to trade in humans. The Romans had enslaved long before them. The Romans had also conquered and settled large areas of Europe, the Middle East and northern Africa, demonstrating sadism in their methods of punishment. In the middle ages, when the Vikings thrived, religious persecution, crusades, witch hunts, enslavement and torture were practiced in many of the lands they visited. What is perhaps under-appreciated is the manner in which Vikings adapted to new environs, integrating in times of peace with indigenous populations. For the era, they also were more egalitarian than many other European cultures.

Jón argues that, as a nation, his native Iceland has its roots in both a Viking and a Celtic past. This may be the result of pre-Viking settlement by Irish hermits, the transportation, willingly or otherwise, of Celts from Ireland and Scotland by the Vikings, or a combination of these factors. Jón also described the resistance of Icelandic society to any form of overlordship for hundreds of years, with an egalitarian Commonwealth rejecting the overtures of the Norwegian crown until the thirteenth century. Archeological discoveries have unveiled the high status that some women could achieve across the Norse domains, regardless of whether they were born in the Nordic region or came from southern lands and had been absorbed into Viking communities. Morten believes that women even played a role on the battlefield, sometimes as warriors but more often behind the lines motivating the troops, establishing a purpose that tied actions in combat to the support of the broader community.

This is not to suggest that there were not social hierarchies within Viking society. As we have seen, chieftains could exert power and secure followers. But Morten maintains that such hierarchies bridged the divide between free men and *thralls*, the Old Norse for slaves. If you had valuable skills, in a craft, for example, you could still attain reasonably high status as a slave. A Viking ship would usually be crewed by free men, but slaves might also be on board to serve the sailor–warriors. Supply ships would also be required to accompany long-distance expeditions. Feeding an army, whether floating or on land, was of the utmost importance.

Lack of food may have been the original impetus behind the first Scandinavian voyages and the eventual Viking diaspora that was established during the eighth to eleventh centuries. The Scandinavian landscape was varied, from the Danish flatlands and Swedish forests to the mountains and fjords of Norway. Yet all were blanketed during long winters in darkness and snow. In around 535 CE the already harsh Nordic winter was exacerbated by dust clouds resulting from volcanic eruptions. These caused crop failures and famine. Cataclysm created a need for action, perhaps establishing an awareness that in times of need, supplies could be sourced from elsewhere, even if taken by force. But this elongated period of darkness and cold also informed the Norse culture that would take hold in the subsequent centuries, seeping into the mythology that the Vikings would eventually codify in Iceland. The *Fimbulwinter*, or great winter, recorded in the *Poetic Edda*, precedes the great battle, natural disasters and ultimate rebirth of the Earth that are the events that comprise *Ragnarök*.

The *Poetic Edda* is comprised of both heroic and mythological poems. Of the latter, the *Hávamál*, also known as "Sayings of the High One", has an enduring appeal, appreciated for its gnomic wisdom. The poem captures values and behaviors that were a feature of Viking communities and modeled by those who had earned respect. It includes guidance on how to live your life and conduct yourself in company. In the latter half of the twentieth century, pagan religious movements emerged that abstracted ideas from Norse mythology, especially from the *Hávamál*. These include Ásátru and Odinism. Sects within these broader belief systems identified principles that defined their religious practice but have equal relevance today from a non-religious, philosophical perspective.

The nine noble virtues provide us with a useful lens through which to consider Nordic leadership. The Nordic nations are largely secular societies today, but they bear the traces culturally, physically in the form of buildings and artifacts, and behaviorally of Viking paganism and post-Reformation Lutheranism. The virtues provide a thread through the ages, reflecting a worldview that is as relevant to the first settlers in Iceland as it is to a nineteenth-century pastor like N. F. S. Grundtvig or a modern political leader or entrepreneur in any of Scandinavia's vibrant capital cities. These virtues are courage, truth, honor, fidelity, discipline, hospitality, self-reliance, industriousness and perseverance. In the next section of the book, we will rely on each of them as a means to identify and examine the traits of Nordic leaders in a variety of different fields and disciplines.

History is always a source of knowledge and information about how to address the present and prepare for the future. The Vikings dealt with great complexity in their navigation of the seas, both previously known and unknown, and in their interactions with the peoples they encountered on their travels. They developed political and legal systems, and nurtured close-knit communities that were networked over large expanses of land. In their military and seafaring methods, they established great levels of efficiency and effectiveness with reasonably small numbers, profiting from their endeavors, establishing new trade relationships and garnering diplomatic and military respect. In the role played on the global stage by their Nordic descendants we find echoes of their success. In the current era of great uncertainty and extreme change—exacerbated by complex issues like climate change, mass migration, population growth, longevity of life, economic instability, terrorism and regional warfare—there are lessons for all of us to be found among the modern Vikings and their medieval forebears.

PART II
VIKING VIRTUES

CHAPTER 3
COURAGE

The cowardly man thinks he'll live forever,
if he keeps away from fighting;
but old age won't grant him a truce
even if spears spare him.
~ *The Poetic Edda*, Sayings of the High One, Stanza 16

There is a vast wealth of knowledge contained in the small but significant gestures that occur in our world every single day. And we dismiss that knowledge at great risk to our future well-being, productivity, safety, and the nourishment of our own human spirits.
~ Christian Madsbjerg, *Sensemaking*

Nordic culture is filled with examples of courage, from the voyages into the unknown conducted by early Viking adventurers to the mythology they left as their legacy. It is the subject of contemporary artworks, books and films, and underlies activities in design, business and humanitarian work in the non-profit sector. Courage manifests itself in a number of different ways. For example, there is courage in the face of adversity, captured in Norse mythology through the accounts of Thor's battles with the giants, a Northmen's counterpart to the biblical tale of David and Goliath. Then there is Erik the Red's discovery and settlement of new territory in Greenland documented in the Icelandic Sagas, or Roald Amundsen's early twentieth-century expedition to the South Pole. Additionally, there are the resistance movements of World War II and the more recent presence in conflict zones of special forces and peace-keeping units, such as the Danish Jægerkorpset, Finnish Suomen Kansainvälinen Valmiusjoukko, Icelandic Víkingasveitin, Norwegian Forsvarets Spesialkommando and Swedish Särskilda Operationsgruppen.

Courage can also equate to standing up for what you believe in, embodying your principles and values, confronting prejudice and inequalities, protecting your family, friends and community. Such a tendency underpins the welfare states of these Nordic nations. It can also be exemplified by making difficult decisions that ignore the short-term gain of the few and benefit the long-term social good of the many. The Nordics do not back away from difficult decisions, even when such decisions are met with bafflement and mockery from those outside their societies. Such is the nature of innovation: initial resistance giving way to appreciation evidenced by imitation. In the early 1970s, for example, in the wake of the OPEC oil crisis, the Nordics led the way in the move towards renewable energies. Today, the Danish company Vestas is the world's largest manufacturer of wind turbines, constructing its modern-day monuments to renewable energy around the globe.

Challenges posed by allies are not ducked either. In June 2017, in the wake of President Trump's withdrawal of the United

States from the Paris Climate Agreement, the political leaders of the five Nordic nations responded almost immediately with a joint statement reaffirming their commitment to the accord and urging Trump to follow suit. A solitary sentence summarized their position, which could be applied not only to their attitude towards climate change, but to their entire socio-political system and their progressive orientation: "We stand by our promise to future generations." Courage is fueled by conviction, by belief in a cause, demonstrated in both word and deed. Leadership is judged by what you do, how you influence and inspire others, how you unite them in common purpose.

A single image from Ingmar Bergman's celebrated 1957 film *Det sjunde inseglet* (*The Seventh Seal*) distills these various interpretations of what courage can mean. Two figures sit facing each other on a beach, a chessboard between them. Antonius Block (Max von Sydow), a knight, has just returned to a plague-ravaged Sweden after fighting in the Crusades. He finds himself confronted by Death (Bengt Ekerot) whose presence he has sensed for some time but who has only now chosen to reveal himself. Death has come to harvest another soul. But Block prolongs his time on Earth by challenging Death to a game of chess, negotiating for a stay of execution should he emerge the victor. Rather than cowardice or fear, Block demonstrates courage. Rather than accepting the end, he proposes a new beginning in the form of a board game.

Contrasts and their nuanced balance are interwoven throughout the film. While Block and his squire, Jöns (Gunnar Björnstrand), demonstrate courage and service to others in their own distinct ways, many other characters exhibit self-centeredness or cowardice. Reality is in constant interplay with illusion, faith with skepticism, love with lust, intellect with emotions, in varying shades of gray. Nothing is quite as clear-cut as the black and white of the chess pieces. The world is more complex than a board game, less regulated, more volatile. In order to thrive in such an environment, it is necessary to be responsive, adapting to contextual changes, staying true to your principles but demonstrating flexibility. Block is motivated by an existential aspiration to accomplish "one meaningful deed" before his own demise. This gives his actions a purpose focused on a social good rather than his own preservation. Distracting Death near the dénouement of their chess game, he is able to save the lives of several of his companions, then accept his own end with grace.

Serving a higher purpose, alongside the importance placed in trust-based relationships, was one of the most recurrent themes of The *Return of the Vikings* interviews. Time and again, people interviewed for this project expressed an interest in serving something bigger than themselves, in finding personal fulfillment in activities that benefited a broader community. Wouldn't it be nice, they speculated, if we could leave the world in a better state than that in which we found it. In his book *The Purpose Effect*, Dan Pontefract investigates how it is possible to achieve a "sweet spot" whereby the purpose of the organization you represent, your role within that organization and your personal purpose all align. This sweet spot appears to be the norm for many Nordic leaders who consistently find ways to balance purpose with profit, social welfare with capitalism, individual autonomy with collective achievement. The survival instinct that characterized life in Viking communities, working together to make it through another harsh winter, ensuring enough supplies were available to sustain people, has evolved into a general ethos regarding how work is done and why. Courage individually, as well as courage in numbers.

One model that enables this telescoping back and forth between the macro and the micro, and the realization of profit in pursuit of purpose, is that of the industrial foundation. Steen Thomsen of the Center for Corporate Governance at the Copenhagen Business School has studied such foundations in depth. The concept is not unique to the Nordic region, with industrial foundations established in countries such as Germany, India and the United States. Yet a particular variation of the model endures in the Scandinavian nations, particularly in Denmark. Here industrial foundations are established, through the donations of wealthy entrepreneurs, as independent legal entities that own businesses. Their governance arrangements are set out under a founder's charter, and are overseen by a board under the supervision of a government regulator. Most foundations pursue a charitable purpose, although some are created to benefit a specific organization. Their philanthropy is enabled by dividend payments on shares held in the founder's original company. A significant proportion of charitable donations are directed towards research and development activities.

Thomsen observes that many founding entrepreneurs are attracted to such a model for more than one reason. Among the more noble of these is the desire to give back to society, whereas a more practical one is the avoidance of high taxes, given the manner in which donations to foundations are protected. Nevertheless, as with the taxation system and its servicing of the welfare state, the money used to set up the industrial foundations ultimately serves a social good. These are organizations that are socially responsible by design rather than afterthought. What is extraordinary about them however—and one of the reasons this particular model did not prevail in the United States—is that the boards of the foundations exert influence through their shareholding on the operation of well-known and successful businesses. For example, Carlsberg, Maersk and Novo Nordisk, among Denmark's largest companies, all are subject to majority control by industrial foundations. In an extreme example, the LEO Foundation owns all the shares in LEO Pharma, with full ownership a condition of its charter.

The Carlsberg Foundation was established in 1876, with the objective of ensuring good management of the founder's brewery and supporting research in the natural sciences, social sciences and humanities. This is achieved via the Carlsberg Research Laboratory and donations to other initiatives. One modern-day beneficiary is Vincent Hendricks, who has relied on the philanthropy of the Carlsberg Foundation, and its advocacy of the social sciences, to create the Center for Information and Bubble Studies (CIBS) under the umbrella of the University of Copenhagen. The CIBS focus is on "information control problems" that manifest themselves in bubbles that can distort and destabilize financial and real-estate markets. The approach is multidisciplinary, drawing on social psychology, political science, mathematics, philosophy, economics and information science, among others.

Vincent and his colleagues are dependent on an initial five-year grant from the Carlsberg Foundation to address key questions relating to bubbles. How do bubble phenomena and social influence adversely affect decision-making and risk tolerance? What lessons can be learned and abstracted from a history of bubble incidents that have resulted in economic collapses and financial crises? Vincent expects that the understanding gained from this work can have a bearing—through adoption, synthesis and adaption—in other fields too. Long-term, the aspiration is that findings from the initial research can be applied in a more progressive way. How can social influence, for example, have a positive impact on how we address big issues like climate change, diminishing natural resources and food supplies, gender equality, immigration, racial diversity, and healthcare for an expanding and ageing population?

The CIBS work draws on knowledge and lessons from the past to explore opportunities for a better future. It is funded by a model that similarly has legacy thinking behind it, with philanthropic donations aimed at serving future generations. At the same time, part of the stimulus behind industrial foundations is protectionism—of an established company. Somehow, as a result of the governance arrangements, these dual impulses sit in easy tension with one another. Steen Thomsen, however, does observe that not all companies are suited to the foundation approach. Indeed, there are cases where old companies stagger on, long past their relevance, because the foundation boards are reluctant to close them down or prohibited from doing so under the terms of the founder's charter. In other cases, the foundation model is ill-suited to a start-up, more likely to have an inhibiting than an enabling effect on its ability to respond rapidly and create on the fly. Nevertheless, there are many "middle-aged" companies—as well as organizations of all ages dedicated to research or education—that thrive under the foundation model. One is International Management Education (IME), the business education institute of which Chris is managing director. IME is an independent, private foundation based in Copenhagen and reliant upon a fund established in 1994. Its original purpose covered the development and implementation of executive education and courses in leadership and management. The articles of association set up an expectation that IME will adapt its deliverables to meet the needs of business leaders. Yet again, the focus is future-oriented, developing leaders that can navigate the uncertainties that tomorrow brings.

Education is essential to another foundation with its roots in Nordic culture. In a global context, IKEA is one of the most recognizable brands to have emerged from the Nordics in the second half of the twentieth-century. IKEA is known for its simply-designed, self-assembly furniture and household accessories. It has stores, adorned with its bold blue and yellow logo colors, in nearly 400 different locations around the world. IKEA is also known for its ethical business practices. When interviewed for this book, for example, Birgitta Jónsdóttir went out of her way to commend the company for lowering its prices in Iceland when it deemed its profits were too high. IKEA was founded in Sweden by Ingvar Kamprad in 1943. He was motivated by the view that "home is the most important place in the world and children its most important people," and by an aspiration to improve the lives of those people.

The success of IKEA over the years made it possible for the IKEA Foundation to be created in 1982. This is the philanthropic arm of the INGKA Foundation, which owns the IKEA Group of companies. The purpose of the IKEA Foundation is to address the root causes of child labor, to promote children's rights and education, and to improve children's opportunities in order that they can take control of their own futures. The IKEA Foundation, which is based in Leiden in the Netherlands, works with a wide range of partners, funding projects that focus on four key areas that together form what is described as "the circle of prosperity". These embrace four fundamentals for a young person's life: a safe place to call home; good health, including access to clean water, sanitation and vaccinations; a quality education, including schooling for children affected by war and natural disasters and a university program for refugees; and a sustainable family income, developing skills that can help people secure employment and improve their self-sufficiency.

Since June 2009, Per Heggenes has been the chief executive officer of the IKEA Foundation. Per, a businessman with a military background in the Norwegian Air Force, had no previous non-governmental organization (NGO), philanthropic or humanitarian experience. In keeping with the recruitment practices espoused under his own leadership, however, he was appointed more for his values than for his competencies. In his own words, "You can teach people skills. It is more difficult to teach them values." It is no accident, therefore, that there is significant alignment between his personal values and those of the Foundation, with an emphasis on people and relationships, collaboration, respect, emotional intelligence and sustainability. His leadership skills, Per contends, were acquired at a young age when a scout in Norway. All the same, his business acumen was perceived as a valuable addition to the IKEA Foundation, bringing different insights to the organization than someone who had only ever experienced NGO work. On appointment, he was tasked with "increasing the giving", making the philanthropic work of the Foundation as effective as possible, meeting the needs of those it is intended to serve.

Per has the courage to challenge the status quo. For example, he argues that there is a need to rethink our educational models, to find alternatives. To address what the next generation requires, Per maintains that it is essential that we are encouraging skills in critical thinking, collaboration, creativity, presentation and team-building, as well as technological proficiency. He is constantly scanning the horizon for change, or taking a big-picture perspective, walking around a problem, viewing it from many different points of view. Despite his Nordic heritage and Netherlands base, he looks further afield for knowledge and data that can inform the decisions he and his colleagues make.

The importance of keeping in mind the global context is something Per often highlights. What is happening right now in Africa or India, for example, can affect all of us. Maybe not straight away but eventually. There is a need to invest in health and education in these regions, because without it the circle of prosperity will fail, and that will have knock-on consequences elsewhere. Everything connects. It is a sentiment echoed by entrepreneur Mika Anttonen. When we look at the world's biggest issues, we have to do so holistically in an egalitarian way. "The world is one unit," Mika says. "The whole ecosystem is one unit. We have to solve the big problems together." The IKEA Foundation provides a platform to experiment without risk. The governance and funding arrangements enable innovation while allowing for the possibility of failure. Christian Stadil and Lene Tanggard describe such an approach as creative courage in their book *In the Shower with Picasso*. They associate it with a willingness to play for big stakes, giving yourself permission to make mistakes, and having the fortitude to struggle on in the face of resistance or adversity. It is a mindset, an attitude, that bears fruit in all sectors, as evidenced by the many people interviewed by Christian Stadil and Lene Tanggard, from architect Bjarke Ingels to filmmaker Jørgen Leth. It is an important ethos for the Foundation to uphold as it seeks and tests out ways to achieve long-term goals that can ensure the sustainability of its circle-of-prosperity initiatives.

Nevertheless, the IKEA Foundation retains a strong interdependency with the rest of the IKEA Group. Per explains, "It is more important what IKEA does than what the Foundation does. It can drive and set standards." By way of example, Per refers to IKEA's relationship with its supply chain, as well as its strict and ambitious code of conduct, which it expects to be upheld not only by its own staff but by all suppliers too. IKEA intends to have a broad communal and societal impact and influence. The work of the Foundation is just one manifestation of this. At the same time, the commercial success of the Group is vital to the philanthropic work that the Foundation is able to achieve. Profit is either reinvested in IKEA or allocated to the Foundation.

While Per had no previous NGO experience, and has only gained awareness of certain Nordic leadership characteristics through working outside his own country in an international context, Rasmus Stuhr Jakobsen believes he has been steeped in the Nordic approach from infancy. Born and educated in Denmark, Rasmus has spent his entire career in humanitarian development work. He has been involved in the United Nations' World Food Program, worked for the Danish Red Cross and, more recently, held senior positions at the Danish Refugee Council, where he currently leads a division dedicated to emergency, safety and supply. Rasmus and his colleagues oversee projects that provide humanitarian aid to conflict-affected refugees and people displaced within their own countries. This includes locations such as Iraq, Yemen, Ukraine, Vietnam, Afghanistan, Libya, Syria, Nigeria, Turkey, Somalia and Kenya.

Within Rasmus's broader remit is the operation of the Danish Demining Group, which has a presence in some of the world's most volatile conflict zones, especially where landmines have been deployed or other remnants of warfare are adversely affecting communities. The Danish Demining Group addresses risk education and community security, not only locating and disarming munitions, but seeking the reduction of small arms and light weapons too. Because of the nature of the work, it is an element of the broader Danish Refugee Council that functions like no other group within it. The Danish Demining Group is comprised of a large number of people with military experience or training, but is also decentralized because of its need to work in a range of former and current conflict zones. This requires agility and adaptiveness, as well as clear division of labor. For example, local people are recruited and trained in how to find and flag unexploded ordnance, some of them making use of new technological services developed by Danish Demining Group. But it is the responsibility of highly skilled technicians to disarm what is found. For such an apparently specialized endeavor, however, the Danish Refugee Council still requires an entrepreneurial mindset among its country leaders. These tend to be recruited locally, with the Danish Refugee Council head office less interested in completer-finisher, detail-oriented profiles, pursuing instead individuals who demonstrate qualities associated with "an ability to innovate, start-up, inspire and lead". Systems and processes supply a loose framework within which to operate. But those in the field are working in highly volatile, complex situations and their facility in thinking on their feet and communicating well with others, both under their leadership and within the communities with which they are working, are paramount.

They are required to deal with the messiness of human actions and relationships in an environment that can be in a constant state of flux. Navigating this can entail frequent adjustments, with small, experimental steps. The need to innovate, therefore, is often motivated by necessity. For Rasmus, the core ingredient of such innovation is trust. This is illustrated well by the experience of Danish Demining Group people in the field in the Ukraine, where they have had to build trust and rapport with the locals to persuade them to adopt SMS, mobile apps and web-based technologies to report the location of munitions without fear of reprisal. As the experience of Danish Demining Group operations demonstrates again and again, if trust is missing, it is impossible to function effectively in times of extreme change. This form of leadership is not named as such by the Danish Refugee Council, but it is Nordic in style, adapted and synthesized in its transplantation to other localities. We will return to this notion of the modification, or the localization, of Nordic leadership later in the book.

Within the Nordic region itself, the leadership style is relatively consistent in terms of its low power distance, autonomy within loose frameworks, collaborative decision-making, and embedment in shared values and purpose. The types of organization to which it is applied, however, have changed over time. Where maritime endeavor, in the form of fishing and shipping, may have predominated in the past in a country like Norway, that has now become oil-rich, with the state holding a majority stake in Statoil. Sweden, on the other hand, has gained a reputation for its industrial output, especially in the field of automobile and arms manufacture. But Sweden has also succumbed to globalization, with some of its big brands like Volvo subsumed into large multinational corporations. Today there is a vibrant start-up community in many of the Nordic nations. Small, agile, experimental businesses finding their feet alongside established brands in the pharmaceutical, furniture, brewing and toy industries. Some of these newcomers are taking advantage of opportunities enabled by the digital revolution, others are looking at big issues related to environmental sustainability.

Despite the lingering signs of industrialization in some areas of the Nordic region, as well as the ongoing exploitation of fossil fuels—which even in 2017 Statoil is extending into the Arctic Circle—what is evident is that these nations are largely dependent on the knowledge economy. Indeed, it could be argued that among their most significant exports are ideas that have informed and shaped human understanding, progress and history in the modern era: design, quantum mechanics, distinctive approaches to pedagogy, existentialism, equality and human rights, parliamentary systems. Whether they are recognizing advances in human thought and action through the award of Nobel Prizes or seeking to cultivate new and innovative solutions to communication, energy, learning or leadership, it appears that the Nordics are dealing in a form of capital that goes beyond the merely financial. Such capital is underpinned by societal concerns and has a view to the long-term.

This outlook is epitomized by Mika Anttonen, one of Finland's few self-made billionaires. Mika is the inspirational leader behind St1, a rapidly growing Nordic energy company. Mika's philosophy for his company and the work it does combines both short-term pragmatism and an aspiration to serve the future. For all the lauding of Nordic nations regarding their adoption of renewable energies and alternative methods of transport, from the bicycle to electric vehicles, there are some inconvenient truths that have to be addressed. This can explain, in part, the unease that is felt regarding Statoil's venture in the Arctic. Mika is quick to highlight two of these, which are interrelated. The first is that the demand for air travel is increasing, which means the extraction of fossil fuels such as oil and its processing to generate gasoline and other bi-products will continue for the foreseeable future, even if electric cars displace fossil-fuel-powered road vehicles. The second is the problem of how to store electricity generated by renewable energy sources. This has not been resolved in a way that is anywhere near cost-effective. It is a huge issue, and means that, for now, the power required for things like electric cars remains reliant on old methods of generation and storage.

Mika is fully committed to developing the means of producing environmentally friendly energy and finding a solution to the perennial storage problem. Nevertheless, the money-generating arm of his business is a fossil fuel one. It focuses on oil refining, oil distribution and retailing via a large network of gasoline stations. The profit made by this is invested by St1 in the renewable solutions, such as wind energy and bio-fuels generated from waste. St1 is also invested in exploring solutions to desertification and reforestation. With the company's overarching energy strategy, Mika sees the fossil arm of the business as the enabler of the strategy and the renewables arm as the executor of it.

Mika articulates all of this in terms of drivers that reflect both the man and the business he leads. Purpose with profit is important: that purpose captures the notion of being a good ancestor, leaving a healthy world for future generations; the profit enables the work necessary to secure that future. There is a steely aspect to the pursuit of such a purpose that is rooted in the Finnish concept of *sisu*, which encapsulates determination, grit, resilience and more. Finally, there is something about overreaching with Mika and St1, about trying to be better tomorrow than you were today in everything you do. This leads to courageous decision-making, balancing the risk appetite of an entrepreneur with the needs of our descendants. In order to navigate towards the future, it is necessary to embrace uncertainty, to be open to possibility, ready to take advantage of new opportunities.

CHAPTER 4
TRUTH

That is the true mingling of kinship when a man can tell
someone all his thoughts;
anything is better than to be fickle;
he is no true friend who only says pleasant things.
~ *The Poetic Edda*, Sayings of the High One, Stanza 124

And trust is what glues together society, the market,
the institutions. Without trust, nothing works. Without
trust, the social contract dissolves and people disappear
as they transform into defensive individuals fighting for
survival.
~ Manuel Castells, *Networks of Outrage and Hope*

One of the great challenges faced by current and future generations are the effects of climate change, its impact on our environment and on the ecosystems that support life on Earth. Truths,
half-truths and blatant lies circulate regarding this most complex

of issues. Advocates for the green movement and climate change deniers both seek to control the dominant narrative, calling for policy changes, revised legislative frameworks, behavioral shifts. Mika Anttonen walks a fine line between these two contrarian forces, seeking environmentally-friendly energy solutions while still exploiting fossil fuels. In this sense, he straddles the gap between an industrial past that still has not relinquished its hold on global business or politics, and a more community-minded, sustainable approach that, in some respects, takes us back to the future, blending progressive technologies with a pre-industrial past.

Mika is fully conscious, however, of the perceived hypocrisies that swirl around these emotive issues. Everything is politicized, the shadow of an imperialist past never too far away. Paradoxically, it is people from countries whose wealth owes much to the use of fossil fuels and heavy industry who now try to change habits and behaviors for all. Their forebears have exploited natural resources at home and in territories previously occupied by force. Today, however, now that they understand the harm, they seek to prevent others, often in those same territories, from following suit. The truths of green activists are confronted with the truths of poverty-stricken, third-world populaces. For the latter, environmental sustainability is not understood as fundamental to their future, concerned as these people are with the next meal, with shelter and clothing, with survival itself, in their day-to-day existence.

Human connection, founded upon trust and empathy, is essential. Only then can different truths, different worldviews be exchanged, reconciled and understood. For Mika, addressing inequalities in the distribution of wealth, in the availability of food and clothing, will be a significant step in the fight against climate change and its effects. As important as finding solutions to renewable energy storage, desertification or reforestation. It is essential to bring people with you, meeting their basic needs, but also raising awareness and understanding of problems and opportunities that can be tackled together. Mika's approach echoes ideas articulated by Jan Carlzon, who argues, "An individual without information cannot take responsibility; an individual who is given information cannot help but take responsibility." In *Moments of Truth*, his bestselling book about the leadership of Scandinavian Airlines (SAS), Jan describes how important it is to emphasize the self-worth of all individuals, to be inclusive in decision-making, and to be effective at communicating, conveying information, influencing, but, more importantly, listening too.

In Jan's view, a leader "must be a visionary, a strategist, an informer, a teacher, and an inspirer". His book, translated into English in 1987, documents his philosophy and has relevance well beyond the aviation industry. The original 1985 Swedish title, *Riv Pyramiderne ned!*, translates as "tear down the pyramids" rather than "moments of truth". This captures Jan's thinking about a flattened organizational structure, with decentralized and distributed responsibilities, fomenting a sense that everyone is in this together, mutually responsible and interdependent. The moments of truth occur when contact is made between the public and members of the SAS staff, between customers and those whose purpose it is to serve them. Everything in the organization is geared towards making that point of contact as effective as possible, with informed individuals acting autonomously in each interaction with a customer. If there is a hierarchy, then it is inverted, with board and president in service of the frontline.

When interviewed for *Return of the Vikings*, Jan reflected that one of the most important changes he oversaw during his tenure at SAS was shifting his colleagues' thinking: the business was not about flying aircraft, it was about people. "We had to move people from a mindset of the industrial revolution, where machines were in focus, to a service-oriented society with increased competition, where the people were in focus." A people-centric outlook applied not only in the customer-facing aspects of the business but in the internal culture too. "This is what I tried to do, to create a clear strategy, to communicate it clearly, and create an environment that was characterized by love and where people dared to take responsibility." This notion of leadership with love is central to the approach of several interviewees. It will be explored in more depth in chapter 8.

Communicating his message authentically, placing emphasis on human connection, became a feature of Jan's leadership at SAS. He refused, for example, to have any photo taken of himself in which an aircraft featured in the same frame, as this would have undermined his overarching message about the centrality of people in the SAS business. Jan estimates that he dedicated over 50% of his time to communication, visiting staff in different locales to share his vision, hear their views and demonstrate their significance to the success of the organization as a whole.

One of Jan's favorite anecdotes relates to the time he was at Newark Airport and, impressed with the service he had received, took the time to go behind the scenes and personally thank the baggage handler for his efforts and contribution to the company. While that individual was shocked to be noticed by the company president, Jan was simply enacting his beliefs and aspirations about the organizational culture and strategy. "Everybody in the organization understood that they had an important role that was part of something bigger than themselves." Jan's philosophy regarding SAS and its leadership involved simplicity, clarity and honesty. What it boiled down to was having a vision and communicating it, developing a strategy and implementing it, never ceasing to listen to and engage with colleagues no matter what role they fulfilled. "The most powerful messages are those that are simple and direct and can serve as a battle cry for people at all organizational levels." Such an approach helped unite people in common purpose. It allowed for diversity of opinions and personal freedom of expression and action, but with the expectation that the leader's decisions would be respected and followed in the knowledge that all views had been taken into account.

SAS was founded in 1946 when airlines from the three Scandinavian nations formed a partnership. It has always exemplified the notion of small pieces loosely joined, a network of disparate groups working together, with a head office in Sweden, a main airport hub in Copenhagen and two other principal hubs in Stockholm and Oslo, with a number of subsidiary airports and businesses in the region. The constituent parts of the SAS family, however, share a geographical location and a cultural heritage reflected not only in linguistic similarities but in common Viking roots. SAS drew on the latter by naming many of its aircraft after prominent Viking figures such as monarchs, chieftains, sea-going explorers, writers and poets. Over the years, the SAS fleet has included aircraft with names like Snorre Viking, Sven Viking, Gunnhild Viking and Erik Viking.

We argue that today's Vikings are the business people, SAS's primary customers, who take to the skies rather than the seas, heading for distant shores to earn reputation and spoils that will make their name back home. As we have observed, there is still an undercurrent of admiration in Nordic societies for those homegrown wanderers, whether individuals or collectives, who have enjoyed success overseas—in business, in sport, in the arts, on the political stage. Hubris is frowned upon but vicarious pleasures can be enjoyed when others do well. As long as they maintain their humility. Conversely, there is a certain sense of schadenfreude when the self-important or the corrupt are brought to account. Tall poppies tend to have their stems clipped, as witness Pippi Longstocking's reaction to pomposity or condescension in Astrid Lindgren's series of children's books.

Sakari Oramo is a highly respected conductor, having enjoyed a successful career at home and abroad. He is currently the chief conductor of the BBC Symphony Orchestra. Sakari is also known for his work with the Finnish Radio Symphony Orchestra, the Ostrobothnian Chamber Orchestra and the Avanti! Chamber Orchestra in his native Finland, as well as with the Royal Stockholm Philharmonic Orchestra in Sweden and the City of Birmingham Symphony Orchestra in the United Kingdom. He ascribes both his success and his leadership style to his desire for inclusion and collaboration, which was instilled in him from primary school age onwards. Sakari aspires to create an environment in which others can flourish but in which he ultimately takes responsibility. In this, his words echo the sentiments expressed by Jan.

"My focus is to create for my players the best possible circumstances for making great music. This might sound like stating the obvious, but it actually isn't that common in orchestras across the globe. To achieve this aim, musicians have to feel appreciated, free to express their concerns, and be a part of the creative process. This approach is actually more demanding for musicians than the traditional one of 'I conduct, you do as I say', where an orchestral musician is reduced to a position similar to a part in a machine." Sakari elaborates, "My ideal orchestra is a collective of informed, active and motivated musicians where everyone knows their place and function and can feel free to have an influence on the whole institution."

At the time of Sakari's appointment to the BBC conductor role, *The Guardian* interviewed his former chief executive at Birmingham, Stephen Maddock. Maddock was quick to commend Sakari's collegiality, his ability to communicate and his subservience to the music he and his colleagues sought to create. "He's a typical Finn—plain-speaking. He's demanding for the sake of the music, but he's a good colleague—it's not about ego." As with Jan, simplicity and directness make for uncomplicated relationships with other people. Honesty, with oneself and with others, allows for trust-based relationships to be established. It also enables clear, two-way communication, setting out a vision, challenging, questioning, developing common understanding.

Telling it as it is, without adornment or embellishment, is part of the Nordic way; a leadership trait mentioned by many interviewees with corporate, government and non-profit experience. Where trust is the norm, honesty and directness can cut through boardroom dances and politics, moving people to open discussion, decisions and action. It results in less preamble and more problem-solving and identification of solutions. It is more meaningful, more authentic, than the song-and-dance routines that prevail elsewhere. This authenticity is at the heart of what Sakari does, whether that is in the interactions with members of the orchestras he leads, or in seeking to bring the music of long-deceased composers to the ears of a modern audience.

It is something of an adage that there is more truth in art than in the rhetoric of politicians, their spin doctors and media bedfellows. The distinction between reality and illusion has fascinated people throughout the history of humanity. The rise and fall of different civilizations is littered with examples of how the wealthy and the powerful took advantage of the willingness of the many to believe in magic or religions or the lies from which their doctrines were fabricated. In recent years, with the Brexit campaign in the United Kingdom, the rise to the presidency of Donald Trump in the United States and the revival of far-right politics on both sides of the Atlantic, there has been much discussion of a post-truth age.

Futurist, author, philosopher and publisher Lene Rachel Andersen argues that in modern, complex societies there is no one central truth, just many individual truths. The resurgent rightwing politicians and activists, however, seek to re-establish a single, collective truth, whether founded upon religious consensus or more secular beliefs. Paradoxically, their modus operandi involves the liberal scattering and repetition of untruths. Their message is amplified by access to and deployment of digital services. Companies such as Cambridge Analytica harvest data about potential supporters of certain parties and politicians. Tailored messages are then targeted at these people's online social profiles with the aim of influencing their actions through the exploitation of fears. They help form the opinion bubbles that are the subject of research led by Vincent Hendricks at CIBS, dependent more on narratives than truths.

The technologies have changed, yet it was ever thus. From smoke signal, to pulpit, to paper, to radio, to television screen. The character of the cheat, the effects of lying and dissembling, are central to the stories we tell ourselves, to our myths, folk tales, sacred texts and modern news coverage. In Norse mythology, Loki is sometimes presented as playful, sometimes as malevolent. He is a shapeshifter who forms alliances of convenience and personal pleasure, sometimes with the gods of *Asgard*, sometimes with the giants. His deception and malice is responsible for the death of Baldr, and his own progeny play significant roles during *Ragnarök*, slaying the likes of Thor and Odin. Truth, for Loki, is a moveable feast. The effects of untruth are clearly laid out in the Norse myths and the *Edda*. The distrust and distortion they engender lead ultimately to the world's grisly end, followed by renewal and regeneration. When the core ingredient of trust is lacking, the fabric of society disintegrates. It is a nihilistic vision but carries a powerful message about community and honesty.

Interwoven with tales of the gods in the literature that has survived from the Viking era are equally enthralling accounts of heroic endeavors by historical figures. These stretch the modern reader's credulity. Or at least they did until modern archeological finds, some of them dependent on advancements in satellite imaging, helped blur the lines between fiction and reality. Among the Icelandic sagas, for example, are *The Saga of Erik the Red* and *The Saga of the Greenlanders*, which recount the discovery and settlement of Greenland and voyages to a place they name Vinland. What at one time seemed fanciful—Norse explorers in the American continent long before any other Europeans—is now accepted by many as fact. A Viking site was discovered at L'Anse aux Meadows in Newfoundland in 1960. More recently, in 2015, space archeologist Sarah Parcak managed to pinpoint and lead a team to a potential new site, further to the south of Newfoundland, at Point Rosee. Evidence of iron-processing and of butternut seeds thought to be from elsewhere in the Gulf of St. Lawrence raise the prospect that the Vikings may have ventured further into the New World than even their sagas suggest. It is possible that mainland New Brunswick was even the site of Vinland.

Fantasy becomes reality. Reality is rendered fiction. Boundaries are elided and blurred. That is certainly the reader's experience with Norwegian author Karl Ove Knausgaard's six-volume *Min kamp* (*My Struggle*) series. Marketed as fiction, these novels are highly autobiographical, intimate in their familial details and insights. They recount the life and memories of a middle-aged man who bears the author's name, documenting his experiences in his native Norway and in Sweden. Knausgaard's books are confessional and formally experimental, the story's flow often interrupted as the narrator is caught up in the minutiae of life. They are imbued with an unflinching and raw honesty that transcends questions about reality and illusion. The truth is essential no matter how it is packaged.

In a conversation with staff writer James Wood of the New Yorker, Knausgaard describes how he was motivated by desperation and frustration. In writing about childhood in *Boyhood Island*, for example, he drew on personal memories, trying to capture how the world was viewed through a child's eyes, to relay truth through fiction. It is what gives his work such impact, the narrator's life lessons and the writer's creative struggles have a visceral effect on the reader. Knausgaard's series taps in to the zeitgeist. For all the political backsliding of 2016, with the alt-right resurgence as its beacon, the years that have followed the international financial crisis of 2007–08 have nevertheless seen a mobilization of the young and the disenfranchised. There is, as writer and activist Rebecca Solnit argues, hope in the darkness, with moves to tackle injustice and inequality. For every Trump or Brexit or Le Pen, there is the triumph of a Trudeau or a

Macron or a groundswell of support among youth voters for the policies advocated by a Corbyn or a Saunders.

Knausgaard explains that through his fiction he hopes to show the world rather than obscure it. The desire for openness and transparency is what has brought together global networks of people seeking the truth behind big finance and government. The sociologist Manuel Castells describes such movements as networks of outrage and hope, typified by the Arab Spring, the international anti-austerity campaigns and Occupy. Small groups in isolation tend to be ineffective; numerous small groups networked together are far more effective, with a louder voice, able to speak truth to power. Many of these communities have made use of digital technologies to connect with one another across national and geographical boundaries, sharing information about corruption and the abuse of human rights, questioning and challenging ruling elites. Yet every innovation carries both opportunity and threat. Digital technologies help bring people together, keeping knowledge in the network, educating and exposing. At the same time, it is exploited by electoral fraudsters and those wishing to impose their worldviews in the most surreptitious of ways.

Birgitta Jónsdóttir has been at the forefront of social activism for many years, campaigning against corruption and nepotism in her native Iceland. She has also been prominent on the international stage, supporting whistleblowers like Chelsea Manning, Edward Snowden and WikiLeaks. She advocates freedom of information, freedom of speech and freedom of expression, as well as the protection of personal data from unwarranted scrutiny or use by either state or corporation. Birgitta was instrumental in the foundation of the International Modern Media Institute (IMMI), an international body that fosters debate about and legislative scrutiny of these matters.

In 2009, Birgitta was elected a Member of the Althing in Iceland as a representative of the Citizens' Movement party, soon helping form the breakaway The Movement party, of which she was the chairperson. In 2012, she co-founded the Icelandic branch of the Pirate Party and, in the elections held the following year, she and her colleagues Helgi Hrafn Gunnarsson and Jón Þór Ólafsson became the first Pirates to be elected to a national parliament anywhere in the world. In the Althing, Birgitta has assumed the role of the outsider-on-the-inside. Writing for *New Internationalist* in 2015, she observed, "Once elected, I went inside the system, to the heart of it, the legislative assembly, like a hacker, analysing its strengths and weaknesses." When interviewed for *Return of the Vikings*, Birgitta drew on the language of mythology and the heroic journey, joking that when she concludes her parliamentary career she intends to write a book from the perspective of someone "in the belly of the beast".

The arts, mythology and a Viking heritage are all part of Birgitta's multifaceted activities and worldview. Despite her involvement with political parties, which has seen her contributing to the Icelandic parliamentary system through three election cycles, gaining re-election in both 2013 and 2016, she does not consider herself a politician. Instead, drawing on her background as poet, artist, web developer, designer and activist, she describes herself as a *poetician*. There is a tendency among artists to gain early insight, to see things from new perspectives, to attune themselves to, even shape, culture. Birgitta argues that artists tend to see issues more holistically than business people or politicians. Remaining open to new experiences has led her to work in different art forms, publishing collections of poetry, exhibiting her visual art around the world, creating music. Birgitta has lived in numerous countries, including the United States, Australia, New Zealand, the Netherlands, the United Kingdom and each of the three Scandinavian nations. She also transformed herself into a digital native from the early days of the World Wide Web, helping pioneer the presentation of the arts online.

Birgitta maintains a website called the *Womb of Creation*. Here she curates her poetry, photography and art, expressing an enduring fascination with Iceland's cultural roots. One collection, *The Messenger*, brings together poetry and art to pay tribute to Norse mythology. Here and in other works, she sheds light on some of the minor Norse gods, especially the women, who she fears are slipping from modern culture's grasp. She has helped organize an Icelandic Viking festival and even developed a role-playing game based on Norse mythology. Birgitta deploys old archetypes and stories to explore humanity and our relationship to the planet. In a section of her website dedicated to myths and gods, she addresses the topic directly. "What I love about this world of Norse Myth is how earthbound it is and how it deals with the most common aspects of the human soul."

As is the case with Jan and Sakari and their leadership styles, Birgitta is people-centric in her approach to art, activism and politics. She challenges the system for the benefit of the individual, the establishment in the name of the many. She appears motivated to expand and enrich her understanding of others, their relationships, communities, beliefs and values. Birgitta is constantly seeking truth: the inner truth about people and what makes them tick; the truth about the interdependencies and complexities of the legal, economic and political systems upon which we all depend.

The political career Birgitta has enjoyed to date has played out against a backdrop of revelations about corruption and exploitation of those same systems. While there is much that is noble about the centrality of trust in Nordic cultures, recent Icelandic history illustrates how it can be exploited by the few to the detriment of the many. Those in power can bypass democratic discourse, making decisions that benefit themselves and those closest to them. The implication of Iceland in the global financial crisis in 2007-08 led to the failure of its three main banks, national economic collapse, social unrest and the prosecution of the prime minister for misconduct in public office—although he was only found guilty of one minor charge in the end. Even as Iceland rebounded from economic calamity in a manner that has not been achieved by other nations deeply affected by the crisis, such as Greece and Spain, it was embroiled in a new scandal. The widespread availability of the Panama Papers, leaked in 2015, also has implicated high-ranking Icelandic officials and prominent business people, including prime minister Sigmundur Davíð Gunnlaugsson, who resigned the following year.

During this period, Birgitta has campaigned for constitutional reform and seen popular support for the Pirate Party rise, earning nearly 15% of the vote in 2016. She retains her enthusiasm for exploring alternative forms of government, society and organization, even as, in the wake of the 2016 election she encountered the difficulties of negotiating cross-party alliances where trust has been eroded. Her hope and expectation is that activism will be catalyzed not only among the Icelandic people who have witnessed the institutional betrayal of their trust, but elsewhere around the globe in response to hate rhetoric and right-wing fundamentalism. When it is the system that has been abused, the collective that has been taken advantage of or let down, the sense of betrayal is amplified. From a societal perspective, it can even feel more harmful than a criminal act carried out against an individual.

In a TEDx talk delivered in Reykjavík in 2015, Birgitta paints a bleak, totalitarian vision of state control, manipulation and suppression drawn from the hybridization of Aldous Huxley's novel *Brave New World* and George Orwell's novel *1984*. Our democracies, she suggests, have metamorphosed into a single dictatorship, "with a hundred talking heads resting on the body of the corporate monster". Countering this, she follows Jan in advocating a more compassionate form of leadership and self-awareness, speaking of the influence psychologist and social philosopher Erich Fromm's *The Art of Loving* has exerted on her. She believes in the power of human connection, highlighting how the web has enabled us to co-create, share, download and remix. "We, the people, are the system," she argues. Our power rests in the collective, in our ability to do things together. Birgitta then offers her favorite word as a call for change and progression: *revolution*. Contained within it are the words *evolution* and *love*. For Birgitta, that is where our future truth lies.

CHAPTER 5

HONOR

Cattle die, kinsmen die,
the self must also die;
but the glory of reputation never dies,
for the man who can get himself a good one.
~ *The Poetic Edda*, Sayings of the High One, Stanza 76

Leaders create leaders by passing on responsibility,
creating ownership, accountability and trust.
~ James Kerr, *Legacy*

There is an expectation established under Nordic leadership that everyone contributes. It stems from the collaborative–cooperative ethos that all Nordics are exposed to from a young age. For those not brought up in this way, more used to competition or a command-and-control leadership style, adapting to the collaborative approach can feel uncomfortable and take time. Conductor Sakari Oramo reflects that he has occasionally encountered members of the orchestras he has worked with for whom the demands on them to take responsibility and contribute to the creative process are entirely alien. Rasmus Stuhr Jakobsen of the Danish Refugee Council observes that some country managers for the organization's overseas operations are uncomfortable with their autonomous roles, more familiar with being told what to do. Such individuals tend to move on from the Danish Refugee Council finding new opportunities more suited to their personal leadership and management preferences.

Ilkka Paananen is the co-founder and chief executive of the Finnish mobile games company Supercell, which is behind such popular successes as *Clash of Clans*, *Hay Day* and *Clash Royale*. Writing in *Nordic Ways*, Paananen describes how over a two-year period between March 2014 and March 2016, his colleagues began development on and chose to abandon numerous projects before the release of *Clash Royale*. These were decisions taken by the team responsible for producing each of the games that were shelved, based on feedback from beta testers and internal quality control. Paananen expresses his pride in the way the company carries out its day-to-day business, with every member of the team assuming responsibility for decision-making and the products they release into the public domain.

Responsibility goes hand-in-hand with trust according to Lene Rachel Andersen. She has been studying social behaviors and practices for many years in support of her work as an economist, philosopher, academic and futurist. At the time she was interviewed for *Return of the Vikings*, Lene was in the middle of writing a book with Tomas Björkman, titled *The Nordic Secret*. In their study, Lene and Tomas ascribe Nordic self-sufficiency and communal mindset to historical influences, including an educational system founded in the concepts of *Bildung* and a localized version of developmental psychology. The German term *Bildung* embraces both continuous learning and personal formation and identity. The individual cultivates an appreciation of the arts, sciences and technology. They develop an awareness of their relationship to community and environment, exercising leadership and judgment. They flourish, gaining self-awareness.

For Lene, responsibility therefore is not only about the autonomous self but about service and accountability; about the individual in relation to and in support of co-workers, family, community and broader society, from town, to region to nation. Self-esteem is balanced by humility, worth in the community is rewarded with respect. An individual who seeks to be a good ancestor honors the achievements of the past, acts with social responsibility in the present, and leaves a legacy that benefits others in the future. This is not about self-erasure but contextualization of an individual's actions and behavior in relation to something bigger than a single person.

The stories of duels, for example, that are scattered throughout the sagas concern individuals protecting their reputation, their personal honor and good name in the community. What others thought of a person mattered because it reflected the value they added to the collective in the present, as well as their social status as both ancestor and descendant. Clear markers of high esteem are evident in Viking ship burial mounds that archeologists have discovered and in rune inscriptions. Always, though, there is this tension between standing out too much, as reflected by *Janteloven,* or tall poppy syndrome, and acting in service of the community. The Law of Jante relies on some basic principles recorded by novelist Aksel Sandemose in his 1933 book *En flyktning krysser sitt spor (A Fugitive Crosses His Tracks)*. In essence, these principles are about respecting your community, not considering yourself special, better or more knowledgeable than others.

Where *Janteloven* frowns on social climbing and overreaching, the Swedish word *lagom* captures a more community-minded spirit. It means "just the right amount" or doing what is sufficient. It is believed that the term was derived from *laget om*, which roughly translates as "around the team". This relates to the Viking tradition of passing around a horn filled with mead, taking only enough to ensure that everyone in the group received their share. With *Janteloven* and *lagom*, then, there is a notion of belonging, being bound by a common cause. The individual represents the honor of the whole community, not just themselves, no matter what the context in which they find themselves.

The Danish politician Per Stig Møller elaborates in the essay collection *Nordic Ways*, drawing on more recent examples from philosophy and art, further highlighting the tension between community and individualism. "The individual must not disappear into the mass, because for Kierkegaard and Ibsen individuals must take responsibility for their choices and stand by their actions and opinions." In trust-based relationships, decision-making and responsibility are distributed and shared. All succeed and fail together, the nominal leader serving, supporting, even protecting, colleagues through good times and bad. Trust and responsibility are both endowed and received, and they help create a sense of belonging. Every action, every decision, can be one of both leadership and service, for both the self and the collective.

Interviewed by Isabel Collins, founder of the culture consultancy Belonging Space in March 2017, Claus Grube, the Danish ambassador to the United Kingdom, offered several insights about his native country that are equally applicable to its Nordic neighbors. "That is Danish leadership in short: It's all about empowering people, so they can perform on their own and to the best of their abilities. Danes are in general very independent, self-motivating and problem-solving in their approach. Danes would hate micromanagement, and they enjoy the freedom and the responsibility that follows. Leadership in Denmark is about setting goals and letting people work. A motivated employee is an employee taking care of his or her own tasks. That's the thinking in the Danish leadership style. We think of education and upbringing along the same lines: Motivation for learning should come from within the person and should not be imposed by way of external pressure."

Consultant and business psychologist Pernille Hippe Brun recounts her experience working with a manufacturing business on the development of a strengths-based leadership program. Her focus was on the characteristic traits of Nordic leadership: trust, collaboration, respect, equality, listening, feedback and creative thinking, as well as communication and access across the corporate hierarchy. Initially, she found the chief executive resistant to sharing personal stories about himself. He was soon persuaded, however, that in demonstrating both authenticity and vulnerability, he helped establish trust and stronger relationships with his team. It was a case of addressing his preconceptions that a leader had to be seen to be strong and professional, that the workplace was not an environment in which to have fun. By emphasizing the human need to connect and understand, the artificial boundaries between professional and personal melted away.

A real test of leadership comes when things are not going well. Thinking and behaving correctly under pressure are essential, staying true to organizational culture and values. On the global stage, natural disasters, financial crises, corruption scandals and terrorist attacks are all too frequent, adding to the complexity of life in the twenty-first century and the strains placed on corporate and political leadership. Media scrutiny and litigiousness only exacerbate the situation. Where responsibility is ducked, fingers pointed at others in a desperate attempt at self-preservation, the fury of the people is ignited, as witness the fallout of the Volkswagen emissions scandal in 2015 or the events in the United Kingdom in June 2017 following a fire at London's Grenfell Tower. However, where those affected by incidents are treated with dignity and respect, another narrative emerges in which honor is forged from disaster. Such was the case in October 2001 when two aircraft collided at the Milan Linate Airport.

Monday 8 October 2001. At 6:10 in the morning, Linate was shrouded in heavy fog but remained operational despite extremely poor visibility. Scandinavian Airlines flight SK686, bound for Copenhagen, was granted clearance for takeoff by the control tower. The pilot commenced the takeoff run. On the point of becoming airborne, the Boeing collided with a small Cessna aircraft that had been mistakenly instructed to cross the runway. The Boeing crashed into a baggage handling building, bursting into flames. All occupants of the two aircraft and four ground staff inside the building were killed, another four people were injured. A total of 118 avoidable deaths.

These are the bare facts that emerged during the investigation of the incident and subsequent criminal proceedings. The investigation identified a range of deficiencies in the Linate layout, signage and procedures, the lack of a functional ground radar system, and the exacerbating effects of the poor weather conditions. In April 2004, a court found four people involved in airport administration and air-traffic control guilty of the Linate disaster and issued custodial sentences. On appeal, however, in 2006, two of the four were acquitted and an additional four people were found guilty. All sentences were commuted by three years under the terms of Italian pardon legislation. These decisions were subsequently upheld by the Appeal Court. That nobody from SAS faced trial, and the company itself faced no legal challenge, was testament not only to Scandinavian Airlines' lack of culpability but to the dignified and honorable manner in which its staff responded in the immediate aftermath of the accident and over the years that followed it.

Roberto Maiorana was uniquely positioned to observe the actions of SAS during this period and how it connected with and supported people affected by the tragedy. Roberto is Italian on his father's side and Swedish on his mother's. He grew up in Sweden and worked internationally for many years with SAS, including in Italy where he was posted as country manager at the time of the Linate disaster. What was apparent to Roberto was that SAS was different culturally than the other organizations with which he came into contact. This manifested itself in the leadership's emphasis on honesty, transparency and accountability, and was brought into stark relief when the actions of SAS personnel were compared with those of Linate administrators during the period that followed the crash. Regardless of their nationality or their position in the organization, SAS employees acted with openness, humility and dignity, working tirelessly for the families who had suffered losses.

In doing so, Roberto's SAS colleagues were following a lead that came from the very top of the organization. Jørgen Lindegaard had only been in post for five months as group president and chief executive of SAS at the time of Linate. It was not the easiest of starts to his tenure in the aviation industry, which was already experiencing difficulties in the wake of the 9/11 terrorist attacks in the United States the previous month. His immediate reaction to Linate, however, was to travel to Milan as quickly as possible. Jørgen caught the first flight he could and was on Italian soil within hours of the crash. Even during the flight from Sweden, he was speaking in person with the elderly parents of one of the crash victims, taking on the difficult task of letting them know that their daughter had lost her life in the accident. In both Sweden and Italy, he interacted with SAS colleagues, listening to what they had to say, drawing on their knowledge, demonstrating the trust he placed in them.

Interviewing SAS veterans like Jørgen, Roberto, media liaison Patrick Trancu and emergency team coordinator Stefan Skantz more than fifteen years after the events, their recollections still seem crystal clear. "Like it was only yesterday," in Jørgen's words. Reliving Linate and its aftermath, several of the interviewees became quite emotional, evidencing total empathy for all those affected, as well as humility about their own involvement and immense pride in the work that their colleagues achieved, taking care of the families and ensuring such an incident could never be repeated. Their actions were collaborative and communal, reaching beyond the bounds of their organization. There was nothing insular or self-protective about the manner in which SAS responded. The families came first, above all else.

It was important, for example, to establish that the SAS pilot and crew were blame-free before their burials, not for the company's benefit but for peace of mind of their loved ones. In another example, Stefan was involved with the repatriation of the Scandinavian victims' bodies. Usually, because of the size of the aircraft used on the route, only two coffins could be flown back at a time. When he discovered that there was a family of four, he refused to separate them. Despite the complexities of running an airline and the location of its aircraft at different terminals around the world at any given point in time, his colleagues responded immediately when he requisitioned a larger Boeing 767 to be dispatched to Milan.

Jørgen shared this reflection: "I did not really feel guilty, but I felt enormously responsible." This explains how he answered questions from journalists at a press conference in Milan on the day of the crash. He immediately assumed responsibility for the incident. Not because there was any evidence that SAS or its personnel were at fault, but because he was the chief executive of the company whose aircraft lay in pieces on the runway, its tail fin still visible, and because he had a duty to support all those impacted by the day's events.

In chapter 1, we heard from Massimo Caiazza, the SAS legal advisor in Italy, who also flagged some of the cultural differences. According to Massimo, where Nordic societies are characterized by implicit trust, Italy is notable for its distrust of the establishment, of the government, of institutions. In Italy, only family earns trust by default. Few in Italy are willing to accept responsibility in public, as it makes them vulnerable to legal challenge. Everything Jørgen did, therefore, in the hours immediately after the crash confounded local expectations, going against the norm. Here was a leader acting transparently, traveling to the scene as soon as possible, refusing to hide away in the airline's Stockholm head office, asking seemingly junior colleagues like Patrick for their opinion and guidance.

By way of contrast, consider the events that occurred on the night of Friday 13 January 2012 and during their protracted aftermath. It took over three years for a judicial process to find the captain of the *Costa Concordia,* guilty of the manslaughter of 32 passengers on the cruise ship which had run aground under his command. In the wake of the disaster, he was accused of having abandoned ship before passengers and crew, abdicating his leadership responsibilities, and subsequently lying to port authorities. Nevertheless, during the period of recriminations and accusations that followed the grounding and abandonment of the ship, as well as the subsequent trial of the ship's captain, there were many who felt that he served as a convenient scapegoat for negligent owners. Where was their leadership and assumption of responsibility?

Or consider the experience of David Dao on Sunday 9 April 2017, when seeking to travel on a domestic United Express flight from Chicago's O'Hare International Airport to Louisville International Airport. United had a fully-booked flight but wanted to transit some of their own staff to Louisville. When passengers declined the offer of compensation to give up their seats, four passengers were randomly selected to leave the flight. When Dao refused, he was forcibly ejected. Mobile video footage filmed by other passengers—which went viral on social media, severely damaging the company's reputation—shows an injured and possibly unconscious Dao being dragged by security personnel from the aircraft. Where was the customer-centric focus there? The honor in service?

Massimo observes that SAS remains the only major airline never to have been sued following a crash. The actions of people at all levels of the company are responsible for this. Stefan believes that the real leader during this period was not a titular figurehead but the SAS organizational culture itself. It is a theme that Roberto picks up. He recalls that his immediate response to Linate was one of flight. "I don't want to be part of this anymore. I want to quit." But then his personal involvement and desire to influence resulted in a feeling of belonging. It felt right, even though he and his colleagues were responding to a disaster. Stefan admits that the experience established a common bond now shared with others who either lived through Linate or were affected by it. In effect, they were putting Jan Carlzon's philosophy of people-centric service into action, providing support, working closely with families, even developing friendships with them. Their work had a purpose; it met a human need.

As we saw in chapter 4, under Jan's leadership communication had been central to how SAS operated, creating moments of truth at the point of contact between people. This still persisted as part of the SAS culture. SAS staff, therefore, sought to keep the families of the crash victims informed, bringing them together for briefings designed to help them manage some of the administrative aspects that followed such an incident, from luggage retrieval to insurance claims. They also fostered interaction between the families themselves and between family members and SAS representatives. Where the families had been fragmented and disorganized before, these gatherings helped seed the creation of more coherent groups, such as the *Comitato 8 ottobre per non dimenticare* and the *Fondazione 8 ottobre 2001*, in both of which Paolo Pettinaroli played a prominent role.

Paolo's 28-year-old son, Lorenzo, had died at Linate. As a way of coping with his bereavement, Paolo determined to transform his personal tragedy into something meaningful. He resigned from his executive role in the fashion industry in order to found and serve as president of the Committee. The Committee involved all the families and sought to establish the facts about the poor procedures and practices that had resulted in the crash, ensuring that those who were culpable would be brought to account. Later, in May 2004, Paolo established the Foundation, which still campaigns today for air transport safety, promoting relevant projects and activities, organizing conferences, seminars and other events on the topic. Throughout the period of his leadership of these two groups, until his own death from cancer in 2013, Paolo was unflinching in his support of and admiration for the SAS culture and leadership, its response to the incident and ongoing relations with the families.

Memorial services were held in Denmark, Norway and Sweden on 12 October 2001 and then at the Duomo di Milano, the local cathedral, the following day in honor of the fact that 64 of the 118 who had lost their lives were Italian nationals. The *Bosco dei Faggi*, a memorial garden, was opened near the airport in March 2002, featuring a sculpture by the Swedish artist Christer Bording. The huge number of people who attended these events brought home a powerful lesson to Jørgen. "I'm responsible for a company that has been involved in an incident affecting thousands and thousands of people's lives." This was still evident ten years later when Chris attended an anniversary memorial service in the Duomo. Thousands of people attended this and other events, having traveled from all over the world.

When Chris took up post in Milan in 2009 as SAS's general manager, Paolo soon took him under his wing. Chris had been a SAS employee at the time of the accident. While at some remove from the events themselves, geographically and in terms of his role at the time, nevertheless, he too had been emotionally affected by it. Moving to Italy, even eight years after the Linate incident, was educational, opening his eyes to the human connection and impact. But also to the effects of SAS's Nordic leadership style and culture. He greatly respected and was humbled by the work his colleagues had undertaken not only in the days that immediately followed the crash but during the subsequent years too. Chris could appreciate the openness of the relationship with the families and the importance of two-way communication. He could also empathize with those who had suffered losses, having experienced bereavement himself as a child when his mother and one of his sisters were killed in a car crash.

Chris's burgeoning friendship with Paolo, as well as his sense of duty to uphold the honor and high esteem in which SAS was held locally, helped prepare him for the anniversary events that took place over a two-day period in October 2011, and at which many of the victims' families were represented. The first ceremony was held early in the morning of Saturday 8 October 2011 on the same runway where the accident had occurred a decade earlier. Chris witnessed another example of the concern for people that characterizes Nordic leadership, disregarding the artificiality of hierarchical or organizational boundaries. As they walked from the terminal towards the runway, the incumbent SAS president and chief executive, Rickard Gustafson, put his hand on Chris's back and enquired if he was OK. It was a small gesture of human kindness that spoke volumes; another moment of truth. Gustafson managed to give Chris a sense of assurance, while reminding him that the weekend was not about protocol or ceremony but all about people—those present and those remembered.

Later that same day, Paolo made a speech in Italian to a congregation of 8,000 in the Duomo. Chris then delivered the same speech in English translation, mindful of maintaining Paolo's heart and conviction as he uttered his words. It was an act that strengthened the bond between the two men, but also symbolized the connection between all the victims: those who had died in 2001, the families that survived and celebrated them, even SAS itself. The latter had proven itself to be more than a faceless corporation. It was an assembly of distinctive people, each of them emotionally affected by the Linate incident, the support they had given families, even the counseling they had received to help them cope with the psychological strain.

Roberto, for one, confesses that Linate made him aware of his own limitations but, in handling the situation, it also made him feel strong. Working with SAS colleagues and the families of those who died, having access to a psychologist and to coaching, all helped change his own thinking about leadership, helped him to be more appreciative of the Nordic style. It also allowed him to put things into perspective, to gain better understanding of people and how they work. Dealing with Linate's aftermath, Roberto came to realize that he can both fall and climb back up again. He found that recovering from the trauma communally was a source of strength that stood both himself and his colleagues in good stead. It enabled them to respond effectively to future incidents such as the 2002-03 SARS outbreak or the Indian Ocean tsunami of 2004.

On Sunday, the second day of the tenth anniversary weekend, the families and other guests attended a memorial concert at La Scala opera house. Chris recalls it as a reflective, near spiritual occasion, echoing Roberto's observations about human connectedness instigated by tragedy. That same evening, a small dinner was hosted by SAS at the Museo del Novecento, a modern-art gallery in the Piazza del Duomo. It was attended by about forty people including SAS personnel who had been involved in 2001, Paolo and a small number of dignitaries, including ambassadors, city officials, airport representatives and SAS executives. When Chris took it upon himself to deliver an unscripted speech before the dinner, he discovered one of his own moments of truth, one that planted a seed for the book you now hold in your hands.

Chris talked about what it is to be human. He highlighted that it is how we act during difficult times, during periods of crisis, that helps define who we are. He expressed gratitude to all his SAS colleagues, regardless of their position or status within the organization, for understanding and embracing their roles in 2001 and again in 2011; for accepting responsibility, engaging with those affected with dignity, honor and respect. As he spoke to the assembled guests, he began to articulate what Nordic leadership means, began to understand that it was an ethos that was more than a regional birthright but could be extended or practiced anywhere.

CHAPTER 6
FIDELITY

You know, if you've a friend whom you really trust
and from whom you want nothing but good,
you should mix your soul with his and exchange gifts,
go and see him often.
~ *The Poetic Edda*, Sayings of the High One, Stanza 44

Business as usual will not work anymore. Instead of just focusing on numbers, processes and structures, management needs to focus on people, their values, passion to make a difference, trust, higher purpose, integrity, loyalty, compassion, their need for togetherness and to be part of something bigger than themselves.
~ Vlatka Hlupic, *The Management Shift*

In Norse mythology, whether relating to the gods or mortals, fidelity manifests itself in a variety of ways. It concerns faithfulness and loyalty to yourself, your personal beliefs and values, to your family or clan, to your friends and community, to your chieftain or monarch, to whichever deity you have chosen to follow and serve. In the *Edda* and the sagas, this Viking virtue—its observation, as well as its betrayal—is illustrated through tales of kinship, marriage, friendship and fealty, even in the face of overwhelming odds.

Of all the occupants of Asgard, the Norse gods' home, Loki is the slipperiest, shapeshifting physically, switching allegiances whenever the mood takes him. He is Odin's blood brother, yet also the parent of Fenrir, Hel and Jormungundr, who later wreak such havoc alongside him during *Ragnarök*. When the other gods discover that Loki is responsible for the death of Baldr, they bind him to a rock in an underground cave using the intestines of his murdered son Narfi. Among the stalactites that hang from the cave's roof, they place a serpent from which venom drips onto Loki's face.

Sigyn, Loki's wife, is given a bowl by the other gods. She demonstrates her allegiance to her husband and murdered child by choosing to stand by his side while he is in bondage. She uses the bowl to gather the venom as it drips from the serpent's fangs. Whenever we experience an earthquake, it is said that it is because Sigyn has had to turn away to empty the full bowl and poison has landed on Loki's face causing him to convulse. Through fidelity to their marriage, Sigyn shares her husband's fate until the time of *Ragnarök*, when he escapes his bonds to fight against the other gods. He who is so untrustworthy nevertheless receives the gift of loyalty from his wife.

In another tale from the *Örvar-Odds Saga*, Hjálmarr is a Swedish warrior whose courage and fighting skills earn him great renown. Hjálmarr is challenged by the Norwegian hero Oddr but the two find themselves evenly matched after two days of battle, neither emerging the victor. Conflict and competition are replaced by collaboration and fidelity as the two swear oaths and mix their blood together to signal their new bond. Oddr is at his friend's side on the island of Samsø after Hjálmarr is challenged to a duel by the berserker Hjörvard. The latter is angered that the princess Ingibjörg has rejected his attentions and declared her love for Hjálmarr.

On Samsø, Oddr fights and defeats Hjörvard and ten of his brothers while Hjálmarr does combat with Angantýr, the eldest of the twelve brothers, who possesses a cursed sword known as Tyrfing. Angantýr is killed but mortally wounds Hjálmarr who, as he dies, composes a farewell poem to Ingibjörg to be recited by Oddr. Before departing the island with his blood brother's corpse, Oddr buries the defeated berserkers with their weapons, including the legendary Tyrfing. When Ingibjörg learns of Hjálmarr's demise, she dies of grief herself, and the two lovers are buried together in a barrow, faithful and together until the end of time.

In the same way that our genes carry our DNA, ensuring the survival of our species, bearing a small piece of ourselves into the future, so too our stories and artifacts. These convey our culture, making beliefs and values available to later generations. Through myth, fable, art and music we create time capsules that bear witness to how we understood and perceived the world during our own age. Over time, some of these beliefs and values fall away, some are transformed, others persevere, unchanging and definitive. The *Edda*, skaldic verse and sagas were poems and narratives that were communicated by word of mouth for centuries before they were codified. In the latter form, however, they have reached us today, still informing, still guiding.

What these stories demonstrate is the fundamental importance that Viking culture attached to family and the bonds of friendship. They were to be defended without question, no matter the cost. Honor was to be found in such shows of courage and fidelity, even when they resulted in death. This is reflected in lines from the *Hávamál*, or "Sayings of the High One", which state, "I know one thing which never dies: / the reputation of each dead man." Loyalty is the foundation of a good reputation; disloyalty or cowardice a guarantee of dishonor or *níð*. A social stigma to besmirch your family's name. Oddr stays true to his word, honoring fallen foes by burying them in barrows. In preserving their reputation, he enhances his own.

There is, then, the exaltation of the individual and the reflected glory that extends to those to whom they have demonstrated fidelity, both giving and receiving respect. In the collaborative environment, everyone benefits. In supporting the chieftain or ship owner who leads a raid overseas, all enjoy the spoils. The followers donate their services, the leader vouchsafes gifts. His success is theirs to share. The leader sells his vision, and the group comes together in its pursuit, united in their shared purpose. It is a notion that scales; as relevant today to family, community, companies, sports teams or nations as it was back then to the Vikings' marauding band of brothers or the small communities back home making provisions for the winter months. Together they exhibit loyalty to the tribe.

Central as it is, the concept of fidelity extends beyond relationships between people. Fidelity can also concern loyalty to ideas and beliefs, their translation into action and practice. We see this, of course, in the spheres of religion and politics, but it is also relevant to the corporate setting. An executive's credibility can rest on their ability to pull people together in service of a vision, a mission, a purpose. If we reflect back on Jan Carlzon's experiences at Scandinavian Airlines, he shared his insights about the importance of the human interaction between SAS staff and customers. The latter took priority over all else, and the way the company was structured and organized had to be inverted in order to achieve this effectively.

Jan had to paint a picture, communicating his vision, in order to bring his colleagues with him on a shared journey. He gave the gift of trust, enabling his team to implement the transformation of the company. As they realized the benefits, they too changed behavior and practices, passing on the same gift themselves. Trust-based relationships and shared objectives helped transform the culture at SAS and resulted in sustained success. In *The Gift*, cultural theorist Lewis Hyde argues that a gift—especially a gift of knowledge, skills, practice or belief—has the power to change the recipient. Such a process is only complete, however, when that same person feels equipped to pass it on too. "Passing the gift along is the act of gratitude that finishes the labor. The transformation is not accomplished until we have the power to give the gift on our own terms." Sharing your ideas is a form of gift-giving; being listened to, being heard, is a gift in return.

A characteristic that many interviewees associated with a Nordic leadership style was consensus. For some, especially outsiders like Chris during his early days at the SAS head office, the pursuit of consensus can be both bewildering and frustrating. Per Tryding suggests that on occasion this approach to decision-making can seem more like an abdication of responsibility, causing delays. The latter is a theme picked up by Sanna Suvanto-Harsaae, a professional board executive, who likens the quest for consensus to turning around an oil tanker. Yet, while recognizing that consensus is a bad fit for anyone accustomed to command-and-control leadership, Per Heggenes argues that it is one of the most egalitarian, people-centric ways to establish common understanding about what an organization is trying to achieve and the responsibility for its outcome. It is a process that concerns belief in and faithfulness to an idea.

There is something about the creation of consensus that is all about preparing the ground, investing time in the right things. At some point, having digested all views, an executive will make the tough decisions and everyone will be expected to act on them. But what is preferable? Taking time to ensure that people are heard, that they understand, that they accept ownership and account-ability, regardless of whether they agree with the final decision or not? Or rushing to action, with divergent interests still unre-solved, eventually investing more time in problem-solving and fire-fighting because of poor judgment? As Chris soon learned, with consensus comes support, alignment and mutual respect. To be effective, your decisions require what the Swedes and the Danes call *forankring* or anchorage within the organizational cul-ture. Sometimes you have to go slow before you can go fast.

Jens Moberg is another corporate leader who holds Jan and his business ideas in high esteem, adapting them to his own experi-ences in the technology industry. Jens abandoned the possibility of a military career in the early 1980s. At the time, he viewed the world as an essentially peaceful place and determined to apply himself in another field where he could be of service. After an initial spell with IBM and marketing studies at the Copenhagen Business School, he entered into a long-term relationship with Microsoft, which would take him from the local Danish market to the regional Nordic one, then on to Europe and, finally, to the global head office in Redmond, Washington, where he was mentored by Steve Ballmer.

When Jens was made responsible for Microsoft's North American sales, it was the first time he had worked in an anglophone country. He learned that, three weeks after taking up post, he was required to deliver a keynote address to 2,000 colleagues. He used much of the intervening period to talk with people from across the organization, seeking their views, attempting to understand their expectations and needs. As with Jan at SAS, Jens appreciated that the hierarchical pyramid had to be inverted. The occasion of his speech was an opportunity to share what he had learned and to sow seeds for future change. His objective, he told staff, was to reduce bureaucracy, making the system work for them rather than adding to their workload. He emphasized the importance of trust between different areas of the company. People in the head office were enablers for those out in the field working directly with customers. They shared a common objective and ought to recognize their interdependency, showing loyalty to each other.

The most compelling observation Jens made that day was about his own role as leader. "There is nobody in this room that works for me. I work for you because you work for the customer." His own demonstration of fidelity to the team was grounded in the notion of service, of servant leadership. In his 1973 essay on the topic, Robert Greenleaf observed, "A fresh critical look is being taken at the issues of power and authority, and people are beginning to learn, however haltingly, to relate to one another in less coercive and more creatively supporting ways. A new moral principle is emerging which holds that the only authority deserving one's allegiance is that which is freely and knowingly granted by the led to the leader in response to, and in proportion to, the clearly evident servant stature of the leader." Like many Nordic leaders, Jens presented himself as a leader of the people not above the people, his status entirely dependent on the gift of followership they bestowed upon him.

Jens describes his approach as "leading from the heart". It is another aspect of his personal style that resonates with Jan Carlzon's own philosophy. As we will see in chapter 8, it is an outlook that informs how Claus Meyer runs his businesses and inspires others too. Jens maintains, however, that in order to be empathetic and compassionate towards others, it is essential to have a good level of self-confidence and self-esteem. It is necessary to balance service and humility with personal well-being and mental fortitude. You should seek to gain understanding of others but also to be understood. Having assumed leadership roles in different countries and regions for Microsoft, and subsequently for numerous different organizations like Grundfos and LE34 at board level, Jens realizes that he has to adapt to different environments. This is not about changing who you are or what you believe in but being responsive, accommodating different situations. To be effective, you have to be contextually relevant.

Agility and flexibility, adapting to context while staying true to values and purpose, are vital skills in times of extreme change and complexity. In a series of articles writer Richard Martin uses the metaphor of the cycling peloton to describe how servant leaders operate in a fluid environment, learning when to take the lead and when to place trust in the expertise, decision-making and judgment of others. The true leader both leads and follows, guides and is guided, teaches and learns, listens and shares. In the peloton, especially over a long, three-week event, leadership is contextual, shifting constantly not only day-by-day but hour-by-hour, dependent on terrain, weather, individual form and team objectives. On flat days, teammates will protect the sprinter from the wind, rotating leadership and servant duties, until they are 300 meters from the finish line. On mountainous days, it is the climber who is the protected rider until the day's final ascent.

Cycling also throws a spotlight on the dynamics that play out between competition, cooperation and collaboration, which has relevance in many other domains, including business and politics. For some, the boundaries are entirely blurred. In the case of pharmaceutical company Novo Nordisk, for example, erstwhile chief executive Lars Rebien Sørensen's passion for the sport combined with organizational purpose through the sponsorship of a professional cycling team. All the riders and several of the support staff on Team Novo Nordisk have type 1 diabetes. As Sørensen explains in a 2015 *Harvard Business Review* article, diabetes is the company's specialty, and has been so for close to a century. Through participation in races and the television coverage it receives, the cycling team helps raise awareness of the condition and the fight against its rise.

In a bike race, numerous teams take part, each with a range of goals and aspirations. Even though they are competing with one another, interesting alliances take shape and then dissolve along the way. Nowhere is this more evident than in the breakaway. This often forms early in the day's racing, with a group of riders pulling away from the main peloton. Usually, members of a successful breakaway will temporarily put aside competition to work together in order to establish a time gap between themselves and the peloton. Each member of the breakaway will have different personal objectives. Some will be working towards a stage win, others will be working on behalf of another team member behind them. Others still will be content with several hours of television exposure for their team's sponsors.

In this situation, the three Cs of competition, cooperation and collaboration are in a constant state of flux. Movement from competition to collaboration or cooperation usually reflects varying levels of trust. The more collaborative the endeavor, the higher the level of trust. If the breakaway contains two or more members from the same team, they work together on a trust basis. Collaboration is about common purpose and shared goals, whereas cooperation is about unions of temporary convenience which can be mutually beneficial during the pursuit of different objectives.

Members of different teams may cooperate for an extended period of time, mixing trust and hope that their companions will do their fair share. Such cooperation reverts back to competition, though, once the finish line is near. The same can be said of coalition politics, with members of different parties reigniting their differences when another election is announced. Competition is both divergent and convergent in that it involves different groups pursuing the same thing in different ways. Such competing groups are inherently distrustful of each another. A breakaway that lacks either cooperation or collaboration is doomed to failure. It is difficult to trust an individual or group that can never set competition to one side.

Jan Olaf Mirko Härter is a theoretical and experimental physicist currently based at the Niels Bohr Institute at the University of Copenhagen. Jan Olaf specializes in biocomplexity, examining the intricate, emergent properties of systems. This includes particle interaction, organization and patterns, but it also extends in application to the study of self-organization in social systems. Jan Olaf and his colleagues have made use of computer gaming to explore the effects of networks among people. Their research identifies a continuum between selfishness and collaboration. The position of an individual on that continuum is determined by a variety of factors that include trust, relationships with others, knowledge sharing, reputation and social capital.

There are similarities in their findings with the work of organizational psychologist Adam Grant. In *Give and Take*, he identifies another spectrum embracing giving, matching and taking behavior, arguing that it is givers who tend to be successful and who are often the more effective leaders. A gift made without expectation of reciprocation earns social capital. As we have already observed, the more powerful gifts tend not to be material but intangible, based on knowledge and ideas. A gift can be as ethereal as the trust a leader invests in their team.

Generally, trust is implicit in Nordic societies. It is baked into social interactions, evident from an early age in educational practices, in the encouragement of collaborative projects, in the social welfare system, in the low power distance that characterizes organizational structure and operation. In anglophone countries like the United Kingdom and the United States, on the other hand, greater emphasis is placed on competition. Trust has to be earned in these countries. Distrust is the norm, particularly distrust of the institution as embodied by corporate and political leaders, but also distrust exhibited by leaders themselves in their micromanagement of people who tend to be far more knowledgeable and competent than they are.

In a society fueled by trust, the state is there as an enabler, encouraging innovation and risk, but providing a security net for when things do not work out. In one impacted by the negativity of distrust, inhibition and interdiction are the norm, with the nanny state always looking over your shoulder. It is an argument that informs Anu Partanen's study *The Nordic Theory of Everything*, in which she observes that the social welfare system in the Nordics enables personal autonomy whereas the US system creates unhealthy dependency and interference. As we saw in chapter 1, in Denmark it is perfectly acceptable to leave a sleeping child in a stroller on the street outside a café. But in the United States such action can lead to prosecution for neglect. In the Nordics, implicit trust establishes an expectation that others will do the right thing. Elsewhere, where distrust is endemic, everyone is suspect. These worldviews inevitably shape different cultural approaches to and perception of collaboration and cooperation.

When Rufus Gifford was posted to Denmark as the ambassador for the United States, he had a good sense of what his own government was trying to achieve but a less clear understanding of how that might fit with Danish society. He wanted to educate himself and, in a break from the protective shield of embassy life, elected to get out of his comfort zone, touring the country, engaging with and listening to its people. Rufus believed that simply managing the strong relationship between the two countries would be boring. He was far more interested in exploring how to improve it, focusing on human relationships, recognizing that this was not something he could do alone. How could both nations benefit further from their relationship politically, economically, culturally and militarily?

As ambassador, Rufus had to do his job and represent his country. But it was essential to him to be accessible, to establish trust and sincerity through speaking directly to people. This even extended to appearing in his own reality television show in Denmark, which was a surprise Netflix hit. Prior to his move to Scandinavia, throughout the period of his political involvement in the United States, he grappled with the question of how to establish trust when there is an inherent distrust of those in power? How to overcome the suspicion that they do not speak from the heart but just cover the talking points? During the Obama election campaigns, he learned that people put more trust in their neighbor's point of view and influence than in that of celebrity political figures. It opened his eyes to the effects of community, networks and collaboration.

Collaboration is a requisite in taking on the challenges of extreme uncertainty, and so too a willingness to cooperate in the right context. The complex issues that confront human civilization cannot be addressed in isolation. Their resolution requires alliances and partnerships that are multidisciplinary, transcending geographic borders. The work that Mika Anttonen is engaged in, for example, seeking solutions to renewable energy generation and storage, combating desertification, addressing reforestation, cuts across multiple domains. *Collaboration: On the Edge of a New Paradigm?* is a documentary film produced and directed by Katja Gry Birkegaard Carlsen and Alfred Birkegaard Hansted. It opens with an epigraph attributed to the Danish philosopher Søren Kierkegaard, which speaks to the mindset exhibited by Mika and others: "To dare is to risk losing your foothold for a moment. Not to dare is to risk losing yourself."

The film was created as part of Alfred Birkegaard's PhD research into philosophy and the human aspects of complex collaboration. It was supported by the Danish Roskilde University and the Danish biotechnology company Novozymes, whose own experimental, open and collaborative approach to scientific research is featured. The documentary is a knowledge journey on a number of levels, physically moving from North America to Denmark, while intellectually blending insights from academia, information technology and the biotechnology sector. It also maps a human trajectory of thought and creativity that moves from the era of the solitary genius to the digital age of networked knowledge; a modern sphere of imagination, collective problem-solving, open information exchange, learning and creativity.

For a society concerned with tall poppy syndrome, there is an egalitarian appeal about collaboration. Pushing the boundaries together, exhibiting faith in and loyalty to the community and its aggregated wisdom and capabilities, cutting across divisions between disciplines. Collaboration is about collective strength, implicit trust, common goals and constant learning. It is about the relationships, not the physical or digital spaces that enable them. In the documentary, therefore, the internet is lauded not for the technology itself but for the advances in human connection, knowledge sharing and cross-border endeavor that it facilitates. It allows connections between people and ideas around the globe to be established, transforming modern science, activism, art and healthcare, into responsive innovation networks.

The overarching purpose that motivates collaboration, the filmmakers suggest, is service of the future. In addressing big issues, seeking solutions to today's complex problems, these innovation networks are demonstrating their fidelity to their own species and its longevity. The point is expressed in botanical terms by plant biochemist Birger Lindberg Møller. "You have to sow and then reap. But today we are only thinking about reaping instead of sowing and creating the possibilities for future generations. Simply reaping is caused by short-term planning instead of long-term investments that are needed to create a foundation for the future generations." In the Nordic foundation model that we explored in chapter 3, we see another counterbalance to the reaping tendency.

The communal aspect of Nordic society tends to be both temporally agnostic and inclusive in this respect. Foundations fund collaborative research and innovation that will benefit future generations. The taxation system supports the welfare state that helps see people through in the present. Meanwhile, national holidays, cultural events and an enduring fascination with the sagas pay homage to historical roots and heritage. There is in these Nordic countries, as Lene Rachel Andersen argues, a strain of positive nationalism that contrasts sharply with the national chauvinism evident in the rhetoric and actions of far-right movements across the globe.

This positive nationalism is exemplified by the pride people show in their national flags or the wearing of national colors at sports events, as we saw with the Icelandic fans at the Euros. It is also evident in the numerous expatriate communities that Henrik has encountered during his time living in California, from the Danish–American Chamber of Commerce, of which he is president, to The Danish Club, the Danes Abroad Business Group Online (DABGO) and the Silicon Vikings, as well as countless others dedicated to the Nordic nations. The people involved share a sense that they are all in it together. They look out for one another, celebrate achievements both past and present, feel united in moving their nations forward, preparing the ground for others who will follow in their footsteps.

CHAPTER 7
DISCIPLINE

Let no man hold onto the cup,
but drink mead in moderation,
let him say what's necessary or be silent;
no man will scold you
because you go off early to bed.
~ *The Poetic Edda*, Sayings of the High One, Stanza 19

But along the way, we are reminded that the process is
as valuable as the product, the method as potentially
revelatory as the motive.
~ Jessica Helfand, *Design: The Invention of Desire*

*A black dot is visible on the mountain's slopes, bobbing up and down, as
it advances towards the summit. After a time, the dot changes trajectory. It descends rapidly, approaching the shoreline. As it does so, it grows
larger, gradually taking on human form. At last, the runners arrive at
the boat that they docked hours earlier. They climb aboard to wash up,*

then return with a tent, which they pitch near the fjord's banks. They are completely alone, at one with the natural environment that surrounds them. Tomorrow they will repeat today's events: sailing along the fjord, landing, running, climbing, camping. Another day in their three-week training-and-recuperation program, the benefits of which will be visible when they enter their next event. Just as their Viking forebears would sail, come ashore and undergo weapons training while preparing themselves for their next raid.

This is an example of an out-of-season regimen that we can imagine a Winter Olympian engaging in to maintain or regain shape. Especially one raised in and conditioned by the Nordic environment. Someone at home in the forests, waterways and mountains of the North. The wintry landscapes such athletes grow up in, the changeable Arctic conditions, both threaten and present opportunities, enabling them to test their innate sporting abilities. An individual aspiring to be the next multi-medal-winning cross-country skier, following the path of Bjørn Dæhlie, or perhaps an equally successful alpine skier like Kjetil André Aamodt, both Norwegian ski legends. As they prepare for the forthcoming rigors of competition during the winter months, they discipline their bodies, developing both mental and physical fortitude. Yet this taxing and simultaneously enjoyable routine of sailing, running and camping is also something that might appeal to many Nordic people: to the outdoor enthusiast, the nature lover, the amateur athlete, the regular participant in the *Birkebeinerrennet*.

This is a mass-start cross-country ski event that is held each year over a 54 km course between Rena and Lillehammer in Norway. It has deep roots in Norway's medieval past; a sporting event as national heritage. Originally, the *Birkebeiner*, or birch legs, was a rebel political group that formed in opposition to the Norwegian king Magnús Erlingsson and his supporters in the late twelfth century. Norway was afflicted by civil war between 1130 and 1240, when Haakon Haakonsson became king and brought stability to his realm. It is the Birkebeiner's daring rescue of the infant Haakon from rival territory that the *Birkebeinerrennet* celebrates. Participants in both the ski event and its mountain-biking equivalent, the 86 km *Birkebeinerrittet,* carry packs weighing 3.5 kg in honor of the monarch-to-be who was carried away by his ski-mounted saviors. There is also a 21km run known as the *Birkebeinerløpet.* Some participants sign up for the *Birkebeinertrippelen,* which requires individuals to undertake all three ski, ride and run challenges between March and August.

There are many Nordic leaders who have a background in sports, among them Bjørn Dæhlie, who has followed up an illustrious, precedent-setting skiing career with one in business. Or the hotelier and environmentalist Petter Stordalen, who used to compete as an Ironman triathlete. Or the hall-of-fame NFL kicker Morten Andersen, nicknamed The Great Dane, who has carved out a new career for himself as a corporate motivational speaker and sports consultant. Or Olympian handball player Camilla Andersen, who established a travel agency specializing in sports after her own retirement from competition. Others still, as we have seen in the case of Jens Moberg, as well as many Danish Demining Group personnel, have undergone military training.

Such people exhibit discipline in the way they pursue objectives, their engagement with others and the behaviors they model. Their discipline is both personal and cultural. Indeed, the Viking virtue of discipline is more specifically concerned with *self*-discipline. It is about staying true to yourself, your way of life, your principles and your values. Even in the most demanding of conditions, in forbidding environments, in the face of antagonism and hostility, whether that is in operations behind enemy lines, preparing for the winning kick in front of tens of thousands of baying fans, or becoming involved in complex boardroom or political negotiations. It demands that you take responsibility for your decisions and actions. In this respect, it is also closely associated with the virtue of honor. There is an expectation that in practicing discipline, the individual exercises restraint in the pursuit of their goals, in following their purpose.

For a decade, from his late teens onwards, management consultant and former elite special operations force soldier Niels Dalhoff found himself straddling the worlds of both the military and elite sports. This represented the fulfillment of a childhood ambition, that had been fuelled by reading about military adventurers climbing Mount Everest. From the age of ten, Niels knew he wanted a career in the army. By his early twenties, he already had four years of army experience under his belt, had uncovered long-hidden sporting capabilities and aptitude as a multidisciplinary pentathlete, and was about to embark on a six-year sojourn with Denmark's special forces, *Jægerkorpset*. First the regular army, then the Jaeger Corps, provided Niels with what he refers to as "the perfect bootcamp for life", outweighing his subsequent university education in Denmark and England.

Military teamwork and his training for and competition in pentathlon provided insight into organization, structure, planning and adaptation. Niels lived and breathed the Viking virtues, acquiring the discipline he had lacked before joining the army, appreciating the power of perseverance, industriousness and self-sacrifice for the greater good. He developed leadership, management and communication skills that he could apply later in life when outside the military bubble. He gained an understanding of the importance of human psychology, of what inspires and inhibits other people. This included the need to show rather than tell, to get your own hands dirty rather than just issue commands, facilitating an environment in which others can develop too.

The transfer from the army to the Jaeger Corps was itself a developmental experience. A six-month application and assessment process was Darwinian in its emphasis on the survival of the fittest, on psychological stamina and physical endurance. A cadre of 86 applicants was whittled down to three, a gradual process that saw the successful candidates going from strength to strength while others were simply worn down and fell away. Niels's selection for the Jaeger Corps pentathlon team similarly represented a step up, with the squad winning the national championship in 1983. As a sportsman, Niels learned never to settle for less, to constantly seek to improve no matter your past successes or level of attainment. Results take care of themselves as long as the individual maintains self-discipline, follows procedure and values quality of effort and outcome over quantification.

Sports and his experience as a liaison between the Jaeger Corps and other special forces, such as the British Green Berets and US Navy SEALs, taught Niels the value of authenticity and humility. While he witnessed some overseas groups briefing commanding officers on one set of "by-the-book" plans and then putting into effect another set entirely, he determined on openness and transparency as the best course of action. Danish forces operated with fewer resources and needed to be more creative with what they had. An inclusive approach to planning military operations was far more effective. With the obvious caveat that the moment boots touched the ground, leaders needed to demonstrate a willingness to throw away those plans and respond to the situation in which they found themselves. They had to think on their feet, act in the moment, innovate. For this to work, trust was vital within the team itself and between the team and the command.

These are essential requirements, Niels contends, not only in a military context but in coping with the complexities of the post-industrial, post-colonial, modern world, whether that is in politics, the creative industries or any other endeavor. They have remained a touchstone throughout his civilian life as a business leader and management consultant, specializing in business development and change leadership. Discipline, he argues, is critical for effective leadership. Preparation and planning, para-doxically, enable you to be far more adaptive when the situation requires it. It helps develop in the individual an acceptance that change will happen, that they will need to respond to it. The more they plan, the more they are equipped to cope. Lack of discipline, on the other hand, results in poor leadership, in poor decision-making.

Niels remains a keen mountain climber and, on occasion, has led amateur groups on expeditions to celebrated peaks. He claims that mountain climbing is the ultimate test of leadership. You have to take calculated risks, always going to the limits, right to the edge where decisions can be a matter of life or death, as was the case when he was in the military. Crucially, though, you need to know when to turn back, when to abandon the mis-sion. The leader has to make the right decisions before it is too late and they endanger themselves and others. Several years ago, Niels set out with a group of inexperienced climbers on the slopes of Mont Blanc. Their poor decision-making, despite his informed guidance, placed the group at risk. It provided a powerful glimpse of what can happen when self-knowledge and self-discipline are lacking.

In his introduction to Nan Shepherd's seminal book *The Living Mountain*, Robert Macfarlane writes of Shepherd's "precision as a form of lyricism, attention as devotion, exactitude as tribute". It is an appreciative phrase that could have been uttered by Marco Sammicheli regarding the positive attributes of Nordic society. Marco, as we discovered in chapter 1, has a familial connection to Denmark but also a professional one relating to his academic and curation work in the field of design. Interviewed for *Return of the Vikings*, Marco acknowledged that when he first visited the Nordic region as a tourist, what immediately struck him was the reliability and precision with which things were done. There was a correctness about how services were delivered, the punctuality of transportation, the manner in which locals interacted with outsiders. All of which contrasted favorably with what he was accustomed to in Italy. Where his homeland exhibited chaos, the Nordics where characterized by discipline.

Marco became more involved with Nordic culture through repeat visits to the region and the relationships he established with his wife's family and friends. He came to realize that the locals complied with rules, creating this sense of precision and propriety, not because they had to but because it was part of their being, a fact of their social conditioning and the expectations that held in the culture. Rules were not there simply to be slavishly followed, they were a consequence of a quest for efficiency that was as evident in the design of the urban space, furniture and lighting that intrigued him as a journalist and academic, as it was in the function of organizations or the training of athletes. In any walk of life, loose frameworks were in place, more creative constraint than proscriptive regulation. These frameworks were intended to serve a need. If they failed to do so, there was room to adapt, to innovate and create.

Outsiders on the inside, like Marco in Denmark or his Italian compatriot Massimo Caiazza in Sweden, detect in these cultures a certain ethos, founded upon shared values, that informs how their societies and organizations function. Others, like Rasmus Stuhr Jakobsen at the Danish Refugee Council, Sakari Oramo at the BBC Symphony Orchestra or Humphrey Lau at Grundfos in China, have either witnessed or been responsible for its introduction in non-Nordic contexts. Sakari, for example, speaks of the expectations and traditions packaged in the music many orchestras play, derived as it is from a period when royalist and feudal systems held sway. This necessitates the conductor imposing a degree of discipline and conformity on the musicians, while still allowing space for co-creation. It is a case of finding an equilibrium between people knowing their place and feeling a sense of ownership and motivation. The same could be said of the Scandinavian Airlines staff in their day-to-day interaction with customers under Jan Carlzon's leadership. The self-discipline acquired then served them well in times of crisis later in the organization's history.

In the collaborative writing project fronted by academic Lars Kolind and entrepreneur Jacob Bøtter, which resulted in the book *Unboss*, the authors make a case for leadership over management: "The unboss is more servant than master. The unboss is somebody who makes things possible instead of issuing orders. A leader rather than a boss. A designer rather than a producer." Their interpretation of leadership combines the underlying principles that define how many of the practitioners interviewed for this book work with others. It captures, for example, Sakari's nurturing of individual expression within the constraints of audience expectations, as well as Marco's emphasis on design and architecture. The authors elaborate on the notion of a framework that both reflects this design and is informed by overarching purpose.

"A good, strong purpose forms the basis for any movement that wants to make an impact. The movement encourages everybody who shares its objectives to join its network, and this infrastructure serves as the basis for action. The structure of the network transcends traditional barriers like geography. It creates space for an infinite number of groups and sub-groups that share a task, a concern or interest. It forms a marketplace for ideas, challenges, projects and information that transcend geographical and other boundaries." This is an idea of organization representative of a digital age, where the hyperlink bridges across languages and national borders, enabling the values and principles of one culture to wash up on the shores of many others. Information technology entrepreneur and founder of the Swedish Pirate Party, Rick Falkvinge, captures similar ideas in *Swarmwise*, his account of the foundation and rise of the Pirate Party. This has its roots in Sweden, initially emerging in response to issues relating to copyright laws. But, as much movement as political party, it has now spread to many other nations, including Iceland, as we saw in chapter 4.

In business, Humphrey Lau, CEO of Danish Grundfos in China, works with a Nordic framework adapted to a foreign market. At a personal level, Humphrey blends both an outsider-on-the-inside and an insider-on-the-outside perspective, which reflects his own struggles of coming to terms with a personal identity that defies categorization. Humphrey was born in Hong Kong and moved to Denmark when he was eight. He spent his formative years in Denmark and was educated as a Dane, but subsequently he has split his professional life between Denmark and China, working with prominent Danish companies like Novo Nordisk, Novozymes and Grundfos.

Linguistically, Humphrey is most at home in Denmark, using the language he was educated with. He is also fluent in English.

When he is in China, however, although his ethnicity suggests that he is a local, his inability to speak or write Mandarin well distinguishes him as an outsider. His multinational experiences have resulted in a personal interpretation of *culture*, which combines ethnicity, the nationality indicated by your passport, and your beliefs and mindset. It is to the latter—the beliefs and mindset—that Marco and Massimo are most attuned in their observations about Nordic society and their manifestation in the way people behave and get things done.

The Nordics have been the birth place of legislatures and parliamentary systems, as well as the testing ground for human rights and freedom of expression, including their subsequent enshrinement in law. Rules and regulations in such an ethos-driven culture are intended to advance human civilization and serve a social good. Their willful disregard, when there is no ulterior motivation to find a better way or serve a greater good, is frowned upon. Just ask anyone who has jaywalked at a red light in Copenhagen and observed the reactions of the other pedestrians. In fact, even rebels and groundbreakers are inclined to codify their practices, set out in a series of rules to be observed by their followers: *Rules for rebels*. A contradictory statement that gets to the heart of the Dogme 95 filmmaking movement.

Dogme 95 was instigated by Danish film directors Lars von Trier and Thomas Vinterberg. In many respects, it was a reaction against mainstream cinema, which was increasingly dominated by big-budget, special-effects-driven films constructed around a few set pieces rather than narrative or character. With their Dogme manifesto and "Vow of Chastity", von Trier, Vinterberg and their colleagues took filmmaking back to basics. They advocated location shooting, the authentic fusion of sound and image, hand-held color cinematography and the adoption of the traditional Academy aspect ratio. Rules forbade the use of special lighting, optical effects, filters, generic conventions or superficial action. Their aspirations and early films were redolent of the European new wave cinema of the 1950s and 1960s, which similarly combined amateurism and professionalism. Their endeavour has resulted in movies such as *Idioterne*, *The King is Alive*, *Mifune's Last Song*, *Italian for Beginners* and *The Celebration*.

The Dogme filmmakers dared to question the legitimacy of practices that prevailed throughout the industry. They rejected the apparent hierarchy that placed Hollywood at its pinnacle. Theirs was a move to the edges, simultaneously experimental yet conformist with their own ideology. A step backwards in order to address the future. One in keeping with tendencies detected by Rolf Jensen and Mika Aaltonen in *The Renaissance Society*, their study of modern and evolving business. The authors observe, "Societies in all countries started as decentralized, fragmented, loosely connected entities with a minimum central authority." Movements like Dogme, Unboss and the Pirate Party validate decentralization and network effects while recognizing the importance of leadership.

Jensen and Aaltonen also highlight another revival. "The old craftsperson is back. He lost his job to the factories and became a worker; now he is back as a small business owner, this time with new tools to compete with the old workplace." While Sweden, in particular, did become industrialized, developing automotive and weapons production facilities, there is an impression that the Nordics missed out on the more pernicious effects of the Industrial Revolution, when they are viewed in their entirety. This goes beyond the visible signs of the machine age, with its environmental scars and soot-smudged cityscapes. It relates too to how organizations were structured and managed.

The effects of Taylorism on industry in the United States and beyond cannot be ignored. Frederick Winslow Taylor was a mechanical engineer who, through the development of scientific management practices, sought to improve the efficiency of factory workers. His ideas coincided with the mass production methods adopted by the likes of car manufacturer Henry Ford. There were a number of consequences that still persist today, affecting many other industries, stretching from manual labor to knowledge work, healthcare and education. These include an emphasis on measurement and quantification, as well as a requirement for middle managers to oversee and monitor workers. There is an unwitting but vicious undercurrent to this approach to work; one in which, conceptually and linguistically, people are dehumanized, treated as replaceable parts that can be calibrated and controlled. More automaton than autonomous.

The work of US engineer and academic W. Edwards Deming in post-war Japan added the need for effectiveness to efficiency. Manufacture could not just be about quantity and output. It also required quality and a focus on outcome too. This necessitated a greater degree of human involvement and decision-making; the use of the mind as well as the hands. The emphasis was more people-centric, yet the labor itself became increasingly automated as the decades passed and advances were made in computer technologies, robotics and artificial intelligence. Meanwhile, managers, policymakers and civil servants continued to value quantification over quality. Numbers could feed league tables. It was more difficult to assess and enumerate quality.

We have already explored the importance of collaboration and trust-based relationships to Nordic society and organizations. Perhaps another reason why leaders in these countries have been able to develop a style that is less authoritarian, hierarchical and quantitative than in many other nations is because of their late acceptance of the Industrial Revolution and rapid subsequent transition to the knowledge economy. Neither can the entrepreneurial spirit and retention of craftsmanship in these nations be ignored. In effect, Nordic businesses large and small are blending different leadership and learning traditions within the region, placing significant emphasis on people, skills, relationships and quality. Efficiency is achieved through loose frameworks rather than rigid control, through learning and refinement and evolving process. As Jensen and Aaltonen suggest, the craftsman has made a comeback as designer, architect, filmmaker, television producer, games developer, brewer, chef, pharmaceutical innovator and digital entrepreneur.

With traditional crafts like carpentry or masonry, there was a lengthy induction period. A young apprentice would learn alongside a master, combining inquiry and imitation. The next stage involved the journeyman years. Like the Vikings of old, the journeyman embarked on an adventure of discovery. They encountered new methods and techniques, internalizing and adapting them, making them their own. Eventually, they reached mastery status themselves, having developed and honed their personal style, establishing their own reputation. They kept the gift moving, still learning themselves while guiding a new cohort of apprentices as they embarked on their own learning journeys. The craftsman acquired discipline in their trade, then modeled it for others.

In keeping with the leadership approaches advocated by Jan Carlzon and Jens Moberg, what a lot of this boils down to is clarity of communication. That is, communication verbalized, codified, visualized and performed. The precision that Marco notes in his observation of Nordic society applies in equal measure to the craftspeople and designers he studies and curates. There is an exactitude and clarity in their working methods. A master requires this not only to ensure the consistent quality of what they produce but to enable the apprentice to learn too. Another Italian, the essayist and novelist Italo Calvino, is illuminating on this point in his *Six Memos for the Next Millennium*. For Calvino, exactitude equates to a well-defined plan of work, incisive and memorable visual images, and a precision in language that enables ideas to be clearly conveyed. Communication itself is rendered a craft, integrated with any other trade that is practiced.

It is no accident that many of the figures that today are associated with a golden age of Nordic design started out as apprentices. Arne Jacobsen, for example, was an apprentice mason before opting to study architecture at the Royal Danish Academy of Fine Arts. Poul Kjærholm, on the other hand, was an apprentice cabinetmaker before attending the same institution, where he eventually became a member of the faculty. Contemporary architect Bjarke Ingels even chose the same alma mater for a more personalized form of apprenticeship. He had aspirations to be a cartoonist, and chose to study architecture in order to improve his drawing skills. Immersion in the discipline of architecture opened his eyes to its potential and enabled a change of focus and application. In each instance, the individual sought to blend different learning opportunities, maintaining a polymathic outlook in knowledge acquisition and application.

As we learned in the previous chapter, Rufus Gifford sought to remain open to the influences of Danish society during his tenure as US ambassador. His own learning journey and burgeoning appreciation of Nordic design, architecture and approaches to urban planning and community laid a path to new opportunities. Through ongoing relationships with a number of Danish organizations, he is helping Nordic knowledge and ideas to be seeded and nurtured overseas. This involves board roles with the Gehl Institute, GAME and Claus Meyer's non-profit Melting Pot Foundation USA, which is overseeing community and culinary projects in the Brownsville neighborhood of Brooklyn. In the case of GAME, for example, Rufus has joined its International Advisory Board supporting the non-government organization as it fosters communal interaction through youth-led streets sports and culture. Rufus is keenly aware of how people-centric initiatives like this, together with better design of urban environments, can benefit US society after his Danish experience.

The quest for and celebration of design intended to improve life is the *raison d'être* of the organization INDEX, where Kigge Hvid is the founding chief executive. This small, multidisciplinary, global company is unique in its tripartite focus on design awards, education and investment across all sectors. Kigge's interest in how business, culture and art can be brought together to add relevance to our everyday experiences, from fashion to food, was the inspiration behind the first company she founded, Øksnehallen. INDEX adds a design dimension to this that incorporates ideas relating to innovation and sustainability. It seeks to recognize and reward those projects that can deliver aesthetic beauty with both function and purpose.

Kigge's aspiration is "to inspire, educate and engage people to design sustainable solutions to global challenges". Echoing Niels Dalhoff, she speaks of dealing with uncertainty through planning, of creativity within frameworks, of the willingness to be responsive and change paths when the need arises. Kigge defines *design* as "a human capacity to make and shape our environment in ways that satisfy our needs and give meaning to our lives". She elaborates that design "is basically music", contending that "we can all make music". Kigge has learned how to pull people together in pursuit of this shared vision, working with diverse teams brought together through similarities and complementary differences. They are simultaneously masters and apprentices in the practice of their disciplines and adaptation to complex problems and challenges.

CHAPTER 8
HOSPITALITY

Water is needful for someone who comes to a meal,
a towel and a warm welcome,
a friendly disposition, if he could get it,
speech and silence in return.
~ *The Poetic Edda*, Sayings of the High One, Stanza 4

It is only with the heart that one can see rightly; what is essential is invisible to the eye.
~ Antoine de Saint-Exupéry, *The Little Prince*

"An artist is never poor," Babette (Stéphane Audran) informs Martine (Birgitte Federspiel) and Philippa (Bodil Kjer), the two sisters in whose house she has served for the past fourteen years. The award-winning 1987 Danish film *Babettes gæstebud* (*Babette's Feast*), adapted from a short story by Karen Blixen, skillfully unpacks the old Viking virtue of hospitality, telescoping through the ages, looking back from a contemporary perspective to a time when Protestant dogmatism held sway. The virtue endures as a quality that is simultaneously pagan, Christian and secular. In essence, it concerns treating other people with dignity and respect, being welcoming towards outsiders, sharing what one has regardless of whether the recipient is considered deserving or not.

The film is set in late-nineteenth-century Denmark. Babette Hersant arrives in a small religious community on the remote west coast of Jutland, Denmark. She carries with her a letter of introduction to the sisters written by Philippa's one-time suitor Achille Papin (Jean-Philippe Lafont). He explains that Babette is a refugee from the counter-revolutionary conflict in Paris, and recommends her as a housekeeper. The sisters are unable to pay for Babette's services but she offers to work for free in return for lodgings. Unbeknownst to them, Babette was the head chef at the celebrated Café Anglais in Paris, and she draws on her culinary skills to enhance the bland meals to which the sisters are accustomed while still honoring the abstemiousness that their pastor father instilled in their local congregation.

This religiously prescribed abhorrence of what a meal could represent is summarized in a *Nordic Ways* essay by chef and entrepreneur Claus Meyer, who has made it his life's work to revolutionize how people appreciate, think about, prepare and source food in the region. "I am from a country where ascetic doctors and puritan priests have led a 300-year-long crusade against the pleasure-giving qualities of food and against sensuality as such. For centuries, the idea of preparing wonderful meals for your loved ones was considered a sin, in line with theft, exaggerated dancing, incest and masturbation. The philosophy so successfully communicated by these fine people was that if you want to live a long and healthy life on earth and avoid going to hell, eat something of inferior taste and get it over with in a hurry."

During her exile from France, a friend of Babette's has continued to renew her lottery ticket each year. When she wins the jackpot of 10,000 francs, she seeks to demonstrate her gratitude to the Danish sisters by organizing a banquet to mark the occasion of what would have been their father's centenary birthday. Secretly, she uses all her winnings to lay on the sumptuous meal, importing ingredients and wines from her home country, infusing its preparation with love and goodwill. While the local banqueters have forsworn any outward demonstration of pleasure in the feast, for fear of betraying their values and faith, they are joined by Martine's former suitor, General Lorens Löwenhielm (Jarl Kulle), who is uninhibited and effusive in his praise, drawing parallels with another meal he enjoyed at the Café Anglais.

Babette's feast has a near-mystical effect on the diners, bringing them together both physically and spiritually, healing rifts, reigniting forgotten loves. For Babette, it is in the act of giving, serving others and creating with love that she experiences a sense of fulfillment. Her wealth comes not from the financial windfall she has now used up, nor even the produce on which she spent it, but from her own artistry and the facilitation of community, of human connection, that her culinary skills enable. "He's a social eater. He eats as if he'd like to unite the people of the world around his pots and pans," says the lead character about the ship's cook Urs in Peter Høeg's novel *Frøken Smillas fornemmelse for sne* (*Smilla's Sense of Snow*). Both Babette and Urs understand the power of giving and nourishment symbolized by a plate of food. In serving others, they serve themselves.

These intertwined social and personal drivers were behind the food culture revolution that Claus has worked towards both within the Nordic region and overseas. As Birgitta Jónsdóttir indicates, *revolution* contains the words *evolution* and *love* within it—literally, figuratively and conceptually. The small action can feed something much larger. A single person's initiative can be the first step in a sweeping movement with unexpected reach. As Claus explains in his *Nordic Ways* essay, the work that he, René Redzepi and Mads Refslund undertook at the celebrated restaurant Noma was about much more than what was on their menu. "We also wanted great food to be compatible with healthiness and sustainability; and at the time, a position taken by no food culture in the entire world." Their approach, nominally under the banner of New Nordic Cuisine, combined the experimental and pedagogical with the nurturing leadership of a movement.

As we saw in chapter 1, the Hofstede cultural dimensions theory indicates a feminine orientation in Nordic societies. Interviewed for *Return of the Vikings*, design executive and serial board member Kigge Hvid identified her own leadership approach as being characterized by a "mothering" desire to nurture, even if she expressed dissatisfaction with the gender specificity of the term. Clarifying her meaning, Kigge explained that she attempts both to establish expectations and to provide support in helping her team meet them. It is another example of where the service of other people is also inextricably intertwined with that of the self. The fragment nurtures the whole, while the reverse is also true. The relationship is symbiotic. "For every atom belonging to me as good belongs to you," as poet Walt Whitman puts it in "Song of Myself".

Kigge highlights how this nurturing, two-way relationship between leader and team member in the workplace is mirrored both in the familial context and in society in general. It is a perspective that shares much with Lene Rachel Andersen's ideas about the individual's relationship to family, community and nation. At home, a parent nurtures and nourishes their child and, in turn, receives succor from them as they age. At a societal level, thanks to the welfare state, the individual contributes to the education, care and protection of others through their tax contributions. They derive benefit themselves from those same services and institutions in their own time of need. They are simultaneously individuals with agency and essential elements in a system that can only be appreciated holistically.

The emphasis Kigge places on the nurturing aspect of leadership intersects with another theme that emerged from the many interviews conducted for this book. The notion of leading with love and seeing with your heart was mentioned time and again, and was the focal point of conversations with the likes of Jan Carlzon, Jens Moberg, Per Heggenes, Birgitta, and Claus himself. The advice that Antoine de Saint-Exupéry's fox imparts to his Little Prince in the children's book of the same name has become a central tenet of the Nordic leadership philosophy. Seeing with your heart is about empathy, gaining understanding, human connection, relationships and the expression of gratitude. It goes beyond the sense of sight, appreciating the invisible, giving space to the sixth sense, the gut feeling, to intuition.

In Claus's view, when you see people with your heart, it opens doors. By way of example, he recounts two frustrating meetings with an ambitious young chef who was seeking backing for a new venture. If Claus had relied solely on his eyes or ears, he might have concluded that he was dealing with a self-important, self-obsessed individual who spoke only about himself. Yet there was something else that Claus was able to latch on to, some invisible connection and understanding. He set aside what his other senses were telling him and went with his heart. Within three months of launching his new restaurant, that same young chef had earned recognition from the Michelin Guide, going from strength to strength in the subsequent period. Claus discovered that he could serve as an enabler but that, in a situation like this, the best form of leadership was to get out of the way. It is the aspiration of any transformational leader: to make yourself redundant.

In other examples, Claus talks of showing gratitude to your staff for following your lead, of how openly thanking people creates a bond. In his book *The Gift*, Lewis Hyde underscores the emotional investment that is necessary for such a display. "When the affection is missing, so is the gratitude." Claus makes the effort to meet new employees, thanking them for their support of his projects. He is willing to give people second chances, too, where errors are made. This applies in his own restaurants and bakeries but also in his non-profit work. One initiative he is involved in is a program for prisoners, teaching them how to grow vegetables, make sourdough bread and prepare a one-star Michelin meal. It is communal, purpose-driven work that helps develop culinary, collaborative and communication skills. Whether as a company founder, consultant or philanthropist, he fulfills the role of a friendly big brother.

Claus is motivated by the notion of trying to find a space where his dreams and those of other people can meet. This is where seeing with your heart, or leading with love, goes beyond one-to-one human relationships, important as they are. Equally significant are the grand plans, the big visions. It is where the leader's role is about inspiring others to help make them a reality. With his prison work, for example, the aspiration is that offenders can find a different path in life, experience personal growth during their participation on the program, and have genuine employment prospects when released from custody. The recent 2016 launch of the Agern restaurant and the Great

Northern Food Hall at Grand Central Station in New York City represent the intersection of Claus's advocacy of healthy food and locally sourced produce, the Meyer business enterprise and a family project. In support of the latter, Claus has transplanted his young family to the United States for a trial period.

The New Nordic Cuisine movement that was galvanized by the launch of Noma was but the culmination of long-harbored ambitions and a shop window for ideas that have had international reach. The movement reflects Claus's sweeping aspirations that relate to cultural and economic transformation, but also are concerned with environmental sustainability and public health, drawing from multiple disciplines across the arts and sciences. "From the beginning," he writes, "we thought of the New Nordic Cuisine as a benign virus, an informal movement of consumers driven not by desire for short-term profits, but by the joy of learning more, and of building true value together. The journey has been characterized by openness, knowledge sharing, a democratic perspective and a wish to include everyone down the road."

Claus considers himself in service of a higher purpose. In an interview with Clara Mavellia of the Cultural Entrepreneurship Institute Berlin, he observes, "Food found me, I didn't find food. It wasn't a decision; it was a calling." That calling has resulted in a rhizomatic entanglement of numerous projects and interests that have taken him from his homeland to France, Bolivia and the United States. From humble beginnings, Claus has found himself on a global platform. He grew up in the Zealand region of Denmark during the 1960s and 1970s where the microwave oven came to symbolize for him both the paucity of the local cuisine and his own broken home. He witnessed his father's abandonment of the family and his mother's descent into alcoholism. It was a rocky culinary start for someone who would go on to help pioneer a new food movement.

To make waves at home, however, Claus first had to move away, gaining the perspective of an outsider and immersing himself in a new culture entirely. This he found in France, through stays in Paris and, in particular, Agen, where surrogate parent figures educated him in the culinary traditions of Gascony. Claus learned that food was about so much more than sating hunger. It could establish an emotional connection between people. "The dish," as he says, "is the closest distance between two people's hearts." Back home in Denmark, however, he became frustrated by efforts to simply emulate French cuisine. His study of New Spanish Cuisine also cultivated an appreciation of technical proficiency but dissatisfaction with what he perceived to be an undercurrent of elitism and alienation. He wanted to apply the notion of *terroir* in a Nordic context, connecting to the climate and conditions of a specific place. Claus was also inspired by the pared-back approach that the Dogme filmmakers practiced. He was drawn by their back-to-basics, do-it-yourself mindset.

How could such ideas be applied to a culinary movement? What would an ethical cuisine characteristic of the Nordic region look like? How could an understanding and appreciation of the Nordic climate, landscapes and seascapes be reflected in a plate of food? What fish, seafood, meat and vegetables would it entail? How could these innovative chefs achieve their shared objective of deliciousness? How could ingredients be sourced from local suppliers in a sustainable way? How could they achieve a balance between local self-sufficiency and regional sharing and supply of quality foodstuffs? What could be grown by themselves or foraged seasonally? How could they remain open to influences from overseas, without compromising their promotion of a regional cuisine? How could they continue to innovate with food, finding new ways to prepare and serve Nordic produce?

After its launch in 2003, Noma became both flagship and playground as Claus and his colleagues addressed these questions and developed the New Nordic Food Manifesto, with the backing of the Nordic Council of Ministers. They discovered ways to reduce the apparent complexities of high-dining cuisine, minimizing the number of ingredients involved, using produce that had previously been left in the ground to rot. René Redzepi, recruited by Claus, became the public face of the restaurant, as it started to garner accolades for both its cuisine and the ethos that underpinned it. Yet Noma itself is but one puzzle piece in a vast jigsaw that Claus has helped assemble. This embraces television shows, books, delicatessens, bakeries, high-end restaurants and a country hotel.

What Claus soon realized was that the word *Nordic* was superfluous to their New Cuisine movement, with its emphasis on the local and the sustainable. Through his Melting Pot foundation, established in 2010, Claus identified new challenges, new ways to spread the word, using cuisine as a way of catalyzing economic and cultural development. As Claus frames it in conversation with Christian Stadil and Lene Tanggaard in their book *In the Shower with Picasso*, "The meal ought to be able to challenge the diner, represent the season and the landscapes, like in Southern Europe. Maybe it could even set new agendas and point toward solutions to problems outside of the restaurants themselves."

Teaming up with the non-governmental organization IBIS, Claus turned his attention to a project in Bolivia, the poorest country in South America, with the intention of applying the New Cuisine philosophy at the Restaurant Gustu in La Paz. Its vision statement echoes Claus's personal purpose: "We believe we can change the world through food." Gustu opened in 2013, advocating environmental care and green cultivation practices. In an effort to support the regional economy, ingredients are sourced by the restaurant from local suppliers who subscribe to these principles. Alongside the fine-dining restaurant, Gustu also has as an educational center, fulfilling a corporate social responsibility remit to develop the professional skills of young Bolivians, not just in relation to cuisine but in leadership and entrepreneurialism too. Gustu runs eleven micro schools in the slums of La Paz and is involved in community projects relating to healthy eating and school meals.

More recently, Claus has turned his attention to a community project in the Brownsville neighborhood in Brooklyn. The Brownsville Community Culinary Center opened in mid-2017 offering a forty-week culinary training program to local residents, as well as eating facilities and a bakery. The project involved extensive engagement with the locals, gaining understanding of their needs and public health considerations. Its opening represents the culmination of a two-year project that Claus initiated when he began work at Grand Central Station. It is his way of giving back, balancing business enterprise with philanthropy, profit with purpose. Questioned about what really matters in life, Claus was quick to respond: loving people, striving to be a better version of yourself and finding balance. As with Melting Pot's prison work in Denmark, the aim is not only to raise awareness of healthy and sustainable eating habits but to equip people with skills that can lead to their eventual employment in the food industry or as culinary entrepreneurs.

Invited to comment on the people who had inspired him during his life, Melting Pot Foundation USA board member Rufus Gifford explained how he was drawn to those who demonstrated humility. He mentioned wounded war veterans, the first gay couple to be married, and the civil rights leaders whose words were so infused with passion. Invoking the artist and civil rights activitist Maya Angelou, he paraphrased her words about how people do not tend to remember exactly what you say but how it makes you feel. Which led him to two contemporary Danish figures he has grown to know: Bjarke Ingels and Claus Meyer. Rufus explained that while both were adept at self-promotion, they managed to remain humble. They were rooted and connected, never losing sight of where they had come from. They managed to convey a Danish sensibility, without being typically Danish. Claus has managed the trick of being simultaneously Danish and a man of the world, finding ways to gift something to all the communities with which he comes into contact.

The notion of giving back, of donating your time, energy and resources for social good, is woven into the fabric of many Nordic societies. In Denmark, volunteerism is common, with people sparing time, for example, to lead scout groups or to help out with the Danske Gymnastik & Idrætsforeninger (Danish Gymnastics and Sports Associations). The blanket term *foreningsdanmark* captures this form of charitable involvement in associations. In Finland, the term *talkoot* refers to the gathering of a group of friends or neighbors to accomplish a specific task. Typically, this involves unpaid labor relating to the community or the local environment. It might, for example, involve the construction or repair of a communal building such as a hall, church or sports facility, or the clearing of a shared garden or public space. A *talkoot* also might be intended to help the elderly who are no longer capable of repairing winter damage to their homes. Where an individual cannot participate in person at a *talkoot*, there is an expectation that they will find another way to contribute, such as providing food for the workers.

In Norway, *dugnadsånd* refers to the spirit and will people show in working together for a better community. Its incorporation of charity, community and tradition is systemic in Norwegian society, inculcated in the young who learn about its importance and relevance early in life. To pitch in and help out, to give up your time in order to assist others, is a gift that you both receive and pass on.

As many of the interviewees note, we have a lot of surplus in our lives now. Working time directives and union negotiators have ensured that the number of hours people work have reduced over time. *Dugnad* and similar communal initiatives place an obligation on the individual to use that time constructively. In Denmark, for example, Kigge recalls being taught at young age by her doctor father and psychologist mother to always have a communal outlook; any spare time was for other people, not for indulging herself. As life expectancy increases, but pension schemes and the welfare state continue to enable retirement at a relatively youthful age, more and more people are looking for other things to occupy their time, for other sources of meaning in their lives. Some find that they can combine both heart and purpose, finding strong emotional investment in charitable work, whether that means volunteering at a club or working unpaid as a sales assistant at a Red Cross store. Personal purpose here intersects with that of an organization, cause or movement.

For several decades, the social philosopher Charles Handy has observed the evolution of what he terms the portfolio career, gaining greater insight as he himself has aged and adjusted the proportion of time he assigns to different activities. Handy distinguishes between four kinds of work. The first is paid employment of the kind undertaken on contract to an organization or as a freelancer in the gig economy. The second is study; the work we invest in our own development and acquisition of knowledge and experience. The third is household chores, doing the dishes, mowing the lawn, cleaning, decorating. The fourth, capturing the notion of *dugnad*, is charitable endeavor; using your time and skills to help others, to further a cause, to make a meaningful contribution to your community. What Handy identifies as personal choice in the Irish, UK and North American societies to which he is accustomed, the Nordics have rendered automatic: volunteerism as instinctive, unconditional service and personal fulfillment.

In Sweden and Finland, *fika* is another connective and nurturing practice that enables the well-being of the individual and the community with which they interact. Viewed simplistically, *fika* is about taking a break, enjoying a coffee and pastry, often in the company of other people. It has been incorporated into the working day in many Swedish and Finnish organizations, with some arranging two *fikor*, first thing in the morning and in the middle of the afternoon. In keeping with Claus's ideas, food and drink here become an expression of love and care for other people. A pause in the day is deliberately created, an opportunity to slow down, to invest time in other people or in quiet reflection, while also nourishing the body. Contrast this with the frenetic speed of purchase and consumption of kiosk coffee carried in plastic cups that typifies the business lifestyles in anglophone nations.

As an outsider embedded for a time in Danish culture, Rufus became fascinated with the concept of *hygge*. It clarified in his mind a significant difference between Danes and his fellow Americans. In Rufus's view, the latter have a tendency to be future-focused, always looking to what is next, pursuing more. With Danes, however, he observed an enjoyment and appreciation of the present moment. As we noted in chapter 1, *hygge* and *fika* can be understood in terms of comfort and indulgence, but there is an aspect to them that is entirely communal too. The individual aims to create a small oasis in time for the mutual benefit of themselves and their companions. A space and momentary pause to enjoy the here and now in an experience that is fundamentally human, stripped of any outward reliance on modern technologies. An example of hospitality as service and sharing.

CHAPTER 9
SELF-RELIANCE

A farm of your own is better, even if small,
everyone's someone at home;
a man's heart bleeds when he has to beg
for food for himself at meal-times.
~ *The Poetic Edda*, Sayings of the High One, Stanza 37

Identities, identifications, and desires cannot be untangled from one another. We become ourselves through others, and the self is a porous thing, not a sealed container.
~ Siri Hustvedt, *Living, Thinking, Looking*

For a group of nations regularly celebrated for their happiness, the Nordic countries have a particularly high rate of divorce. Denmark leads the way with almost every second marriage breaking up, leaving Sweden and Finland not far behind. The practice can be traced back to Viking times and is documented in texts such as the *Laxardal Saga* in which Gudrun divorces Thorvald. Some Viking partners even had their equivalent of a contemporary pre-nuptial agreement, outlining how a divorce would be conducted and the possessions shared. Rather than suggesting a tear in the social fabric, however, it indicates a return to the social commons and a marker of individuality and self-sufficiency, even in the context of the broader community of which each person is an integral element.

This notion picks up a theme that has been raised elsewhere in the book, but requires a little unpacking. There are inherent tensions here. Most overtly between the individual and the collective, but also between a society founded upon trust-based relationships and one that evidences the frequent disintegration and reconfiguration of those relationships. The breakdown and healing of relationships, perversely, can result in the strengthening of trust and bonds. It is a pattern that we can see replicated not only at a personal level in the rites of passage signified by marriage, divorce and remarriage, but commercially in the partnerships involving different companies, and internationally in the treaties and alliances between countries.

The history of the Nordic region from the post-Viking era to the middle of the last century is one of flux and change. Borders shift, monarchies are shared, unions are formed and then disbanded, imperialist impulses result in land grabs and subsequent losses, independence is sought and eventually attained. In 1397, for example, Denmark, Norway and Sweden were brought together in the Kalmar Union under the monarchy of Queen Margaret I. As part of this union, the three nations relinquished sovereignty but not independence. There was, however, a perceived imbalance in the relationship in favor of Denmark, with

Sweden attempting to break away on a number of occasions. This ultimately resulted in the dissolution of the union in 1523. While a union between Denmark and Norway continued, Sweden emerged as the more dominant regional nation during the period that followed, the Protestant Reformation. The defeat of Denmark's army by Holy Roman Empire forces at the Battle of Lutter am Barenberge in 1626 signaled a turning point in the balance of power. Sweden had taken over Finland during the twelfth and thirteenth centuries and began to expand into the area we now know as the Baltic States. As a consequence of military engagement and treaties, Sweden also gradually began to take possession of territories previously held by Denmark. These included since 1645 Halland and Gotland and since 1658 Blekinge and Scania.

The Danish–Norwegian union ended during the Napoleonic Wars in 1814, when Norway was ceded to the king of Sweden under the terms of the Treaty of Kiel. As part of the separation agreement, Denmark retained the former Norwegian territories of Iceland, the Faroe Islands and Greenland. Despite attempts at independence and a constitution that was inspired by the revolutionary models provided by the United States and France, Norway eventually entered into a union with Sweden, which was resolved peacefully in 1905 when Norway gained its independence.

Finland meanwhile was a site of frequent conflict between Sweden and Russia. In the wake of the Finnish War of 1808–09, the autonomous Grand Duchy of Finland was created from Swedish territory, forming part of the expanded Russian Empire for the next century. Prompted by the October Revolution in Russia, however, Finland declared its independence late in 1917. A new border was eventually agreed with the Treaty of Tartu in 1920 following a short-lived conflict with its neighbor and a civil war that raged between January and May 1918. The latter involved foreign powers too, with Soviet Russia backing the socialist Reds and the victorious White Army receiving the support of German troops as well as volunteers from Sweden, Estonia and Poland.

The last of the Nordic nations to achieve independence was Iceland in 1944. Like Finland, it too became a republic, whereas Denmark, Norway and Sweden retained their monarchies. Today, the Faroe Islands and Greenland remain autonomous countries within the Kingdom of Denmark, while Åland is an autonomous, Swedish-speaking region that lies within the Republic of Finland. All these territories and nations became either full or associate members of the Nordic Council, which fosters inter-parliamentary cooperation in the regions. This is supplemented by the Nordic Council of Ministers whose remit focuses on inter-governmental cooperation. The uneasy unions of the past have been transformed in the modern, democratic age into interdependencies made through choice rather than imposition. These countries stand alone, and they stand together, a chaotic past now reconfigured in strong bonds and shared purpose. As Margaret Wheatley puts it, "order exists within disorder and disorder within order."

Wheatley is a management consultant who studies organizational behavior and leadership. She has spent decades applying lessons from the sciences in a business and organizational context. Wheatley draws on biology, chemistry, information theory, quantum physics, chaos theory and systems thinking to improve her understanding of people and how they organize themselves. It has led her to acknowledge a similar tension between the fragment and the whole in her book *Leadership and the New Science*.

"There is another important paradox in living systems: Each organism maintains a clear sense of its individual identity within a larger network of relationships that help shape its identity. Each being is noticeable as a separate entity, yet it is simultaneously part of a whole system." This is helpful in understanding the Viking virtue of self-reliance and the manner in which it persists in contemporary society, manifested in individual action and behavior but also in that of entire nations in terms of their international relations and partnerships.

A Viking was deeply committed to their family, their shipmates and allies in battle. But they desired to be free of dependency, their reputation earned through their own actions rather than the reflected glory of others. It was necessary that they contributed, whether that was in battle, in farming or with craftsmanship. They enjoyed a status in the community because what they did made that community better. The Viking was self-directed, following their own will, electing to serve those around them. Wheatley's lessons from science are again illuminating on this point: "Yet it is very important to note that in all life, the self is not a selfish individual. 'Self' includes awareness of those others it must relate to as part of its system." She elaborates in her book *Finding Our Way,* in an essay co-authored with Myron Rogers: "As systems form, the paradox of individualism and connectedness becomes clearer. Individuals are figuring out how to be together in ways that support themselves. Yet these individuals remain astutely aware of their neighbors and local environmental conditions."

For Vikings, sharing the spoils of raids and warfare was part of the social contract with your community. But frugality in the management of your household was valued too. Storing what foodstuffs and clothing you had, in order to make it through the winter, taking only a small draft in order that others could enjoy their share of mead, speaking only when wisdom could be added to the conversation; all of these are lauded in the literature handed down from the Viking age. Today, personal identity is similarly entangled with exercising free will and providing for others, whether supporting a family, engaging in charitable activity or enabling the welfare state through tax contributions. What the individual does affects the whole system.

The folk high school tradition initially established in Denmark by N. F. S. Grundtvig fostered this dual emphasis on collectivism and mutual self-sufficiency. As Lene Rachel Andersen argues, there was in the beginning of the 20th century a great awakening of the poor, of people who traditionally had been denied an education beyond their teens. Through folk high schools, they acquired moral courage, responsibility and a sense of self in relation to the community and their nation. They acquired an understanding of how they fit in the whole system, seeing the world with new eyes. In a telling observation regarding contemporary society, Marco Sammicheli notes that a trait shared by both the Nordic people he knows and outsiders who have chosen to move to the region relates to doing things on their own terms. They demonstrate self-sufficiency, having a tendency to sort things out themselves rather than relying on others for input, advice or action. Yet, however individualistic their motives, what they do tends to impact those that surround them, sometimes in the most tangential of ways. The Grundtvig effect persists.

Hrútar (*Rams*) is a comic Icelandic film about two brothers and the sheep-farming community of which they are members. Although they live in adjacent houses on land inherited from their parents, the brothers' relationship has broken down and they have not spoken to one another for decades. The sheep they breed, first brought to Iceland by the Vikings as a source of clothing, meat and milk, connect the brothers to long-standing traditions now under threat as modern Icelanders have migrated to the cities and towns and away from rural communities. The fragility of their way of life is highlighted when Gummi (Sigurður Sigurjónsson) discovers that the prize-winning ram owned by his brother Kiddi (Theodór Júlíusson) has contracted scrapie. As a consequence, all the sheep in the valley have to be destroyed, all the farms cleansed and left idle for a period of time, prompting some of the younger members of the community to give up on farming entirely.

Like their nation itself, Gummi and Kiddi are their own islands, solitary and independent. They save their words for their sheep, limiting interaction with other humans, as far as possible, to deeds rather than speech. Gummi, for example, first alerts his brother to problems with his flock with gestures as he walks away from his house. Later in the film he delivers the stricken Kiddi to a hospital by scooping him up with a tractor shovel, transporting him to the nearest town, and dumping him at the entrance. Words are superfluous to requirements. Gummi also takes it on himself to kill his own flock rather than let the biohazards team do it. Kiddi, in turn, acts with drink-fueled anger and violence, first when his brother alerts the authorities to the scrapie outbreak, and later when Gummi takes on the responsibility of sanitizing Kiddi's farm while the latter is incapacitated in hospital. Shooting at his brother's windows is a more powerful statement than any curse he can throw.

Anger and despair break the silence maintained by the brothers for so long. When Kiddi discovers that Gummi has hidden a ram and some ewes apparently unaffected by scrapie in his basement, his initial offer to help preserve the flock is rejected. But when a member of the biohazards team makes the same discovery, the brothers are forced into collaborative action, racing into the mountains on a quad bike, towing the sheep into blizzard conditions. The film ends on a note of reconciliation and the restoration of fraternal affection, as Kiddi hugs the hypothermic Gummi, trying to restore warmth to his body while they shelter from the storm in an ice cave. The island has reconnected to its neighbors, having learned that it is possible to be self-sufficient without being isolated.

Another recent film, adapted from a book by Swedish novelist Fredrik Backman, illustrates how community can resist the individual's urge to withdraw and wall themselves off. "You're amazingly crap at dying," Parvaneh (Bahar Pars) affectionately informs the eponymous curmudgeon played by Rolf Lassgård in *En man som heter Ove* (*A Man Called Ove*). Bereft after the death of his wife Sonja (Ida Engvoll), Ove Lindahl determines to join her in the afterlife. But every attempt to commit suicide is bungled or interrupted by neighbors who pull Ove back into their community, demonstrating their dependency on him, providing him with a sense of belonging and usefulness.

Death, misfortune and misunderstanding have been a mainstay throughout Ove's life, creating a sense of isolation, of battling constantly against the world around him, particularly the "white collar" administrators. This begins with his mother's death when a young child, and is followed by his father's workplace demise and the loss of the family home to fire. The disasters continue when a coach crash while on holiday in Spain results in Sonja being confined to a wheelchair for the rest of her life and the termination of her pregnancy. The sequence culminates with Sonja's death from cancer and Ove's own dismissal from a job he has held for forty years. Such a cursory summary paints a gloomy picture of what is in fact a touching comedy about the warmth of human connection, highlighting the fine balance Nordic artists achieve between melancholia and humor.

When the Iranian immigrant Parvaneh, her Swedish husband and their two young daughters move into the house opposite, Ove discovers that his self-reliance, his knowledge, skills and capabilities can be put in service of others. His burgeoning friendship with Parvaneh has a catalytic effect, seeing him not only assisting with maintenance and childminding chores in her home, or helping her learn to drive, but also beginning to support others in the neighborhood, repairing a bicycle, taking in a young man whose father is unable to accept his homosexuality, adopting a stray cat. He is transformed from the self-appointed community policeman to an avuncular local handyman and activist. He does good for others in the same way that his wife used to do in her capacity as a teacher at the local school, helping young people with learning difficulties.

Throughout, the film lampoons the false tribalism that keeps people apart, revealing the essential humanity that bridges across superficial examples of differentiation. White collars and blue collars. Native Swedes and immigrants. Heterosexuals and homosexuals. Able-bodied and disabled. As in *Rams*, at the heart of *A Man Called Ove* is a tale of two people once close to one another who were transformed into taciturn adversaries. When young men, Ove and Rune (Björe Lundberg) connected on their shared interests, especially their love of rules and regulations, but found their friendship strained by one significant anomaly: Ove's affiliation to the Saab car brand and Rune's to Volvo. This difference is amplified by Rune's replacement of Ove as the head of the neighborhood association, with the final blow delivered when Rune purchases a German BMW.

Ove's reconnection to life and the neighborhood that Parvaneh and her family have facilitated ultimately leads to reconciliation. Ove puts aside his simmering resentment of Rune, now invalided because of a stroke, and his wife Anita (Chatarina Larsson). He works on their behalf to prevent Rune from being taken into a care home against their will and mobilizes the local community to support them. Having spent much of the film visiting his wife's grave and talking to an unresponsive tombstone, he now finds a more receptive figure in Rune. Even if the latter is unable to respond with words, he does so in other ways, with smiles, his eyes and small hand movements. The film ends with Ove, reintegrated into the neighborhood he once cherished, able to die peacefully in his sleep rather than by his own hand. The crowd that gathers for his memorial service reflects all the lives this apparently isolated figure touched. The actions of one impacting on the system as a whole.

While Ove's story is one of a community unwilling to let go of one of its own, for all of his individualistic tendencies, there are occasions where separation is essential for the well-being of one or more of the parties involved. It allows for new beginnings, for reinvention. This was Henrik's experience during his time with the enterprise software company Navision, prior to its acquisition by Microsoft. When Henrik assumed responsibility for managing the relationship with a poorly performing Australian distributor, he rapidly came to the conclusion that he needed to relocate to Brisbane in order to collaborate in proximity rather than at a distance with his new colleagues. What he discovered came as a culture shock: a toxic environment caused by a bullying boss and employees stymied by fear. A community, in other words, seeking to eject the cause of malaise that resided at its core.

This organizational experience was unlike anything Henrik had previously encountered. Although nominally a partner in Navision's business venture in Australia, this co-owner of the distribution company shared none of the Nordic company's ethos. Their leadership style was to withhold trust and apportion blame, competing rather than collaborating, always putting themselves before others. What soon became apparent was that there was a conflict of interest too, with the leader directing a disproportionate number of business leads to another company that they owned. Having ascertained the facts, Henrik had open and constructive discussions with colleagues back home. He guided the executive leadership team in Denmark through negotiations that removed a problem from their Antipodean operation, strengthening their position and making the Australian branch of the business more self-reliant.

With the divorce from a troublesome partner secured, the next step for Henrik was to involve himself in embedding a new leadership style and culture within the company, one that valued and respected people no matter their job title or status. He assumed the role of interim managing director for the next eighteen months, working alongside his Australian successor for the last six of them. With the same personnel in place, motivated by a shared vision for the organization's future progress, and by the faith and trust now placed in them, Navision experienced a remarkable turnaround of fortunes in Australia. Broken relationships with customers were restored, sales increased significantly, and a previously downtrodden team bloomed. Towards the end of his tenure, Henrik was given some of the most powerful feedback he ever received when a colleague's spouse thanked him for setting their partner free to fulfill their potential and achieve their professional ambitions.

For Henrik, he had simply been practicing what he had always known as someone who had been schooled in Denmark, received military training there and worked for Danish organizations. But this feedback prompted him to reflect further on how he had introduced Nordic ideas into a new environment, experiencing spectacular success as a consequence, not only in terms of business results, but in how his colleagues now approached work and interacted with one another. This experience of being an exporter of a Nordic concept about leadership and organizational dynamics, of adapting them to fit different contexts, of helping others with their learning and development as they took on board the new ways of working, is something shared by several interviewees for *Return of the Vikings*.

As Chris discovered when he first moved to the Scandinavian Airlines head office, working for a Nordic organization in a Nordic country, not only are you expected to have an opinion, you are expected to be willing to share it no matter who you are talking to or what their position is. This has a positive effect on how the organization functions, encouraging openness and transparency. When your opinion is required and is taken into consideration during the decision-making process, it gives you a greater sense of involvement and ownership. You can see how you add value, even when decisions do not go your way. It is easier to action decisions and be accountable for their outcome when you know you have been heard. What is normal in the Nordics, however, can seem alien and uncomfortable elsewhere, especially if what you are familiar with is a command-and-control leadership style and deference to hierarchical status and job title.

Anders Fogh Rasmussen experienced something of a dichotomy when he took on the role of Secretary General of NATO between August 2009 and October 2014. While Prime Minister of

Denmark from 2001 to 2009, Anders had often been criticized for being too centralized in his approach to leadership and government. However, when he assumed his new role in a global organization, the opposite was the case, with his modus operandi initially meeting resistance because of its openness and inclusivity. Even his moderate Nordic leadership style prompted discomfort among middle managers who feared a loss of control.

At Microsoft, Jens Moberg had stayed true to his personal ethos about communication and inclusion. Anders sought to replicate this in NATO. The self-reliance and autonomous thinking of the individual was of far greater benefit to the organization than a group of people simply waiting to be told what to do. Knowledge and expertise resided in the network rather than with the person who commanded the largest salary or had the biggest office. Eventually, Anders succeeded in his aim of loosening up the hierarchy and creating a more relaxed atmosphere in meetings. By adapting his methods, he was able to bring the initial critics with him, helping them to appreciate the benefits of inviting others from across the organization to contribute. Fear gave way to mutual appreciation.

Lederne, a Danish professional organization for leaders, conducted a survey of Nordic leaders in the first half of 2017. Their analysis of feedback about leading overseas chimes with Anders's experience and that of other individuals interviewed for this book. Helle Bruun Madsen, executive coach and consultant at Lederne, observes that "it is a good idea to familiarize yourself with the leadership styles that prevail in the countries concerned. It is not everyone who is used to—or prefers—the high degree of freedom and responsibility we have in Nordic organizations. As a leader, you must always adapt your management style to each employee type and find out how they are motivated to perform to their best."

What Anders went through in NATO represents a template for anyone transitioning from a Nordic culture to the bureaucracy and organizational structures of large, monolithic, global bodies. Anders's experiences are echoed by Rasmus Stuhr Jacobsen, for example, who spent time with the United Nations World Food Program. He found the UN unwieldy, overly formal and inhibited by power games. Although he did recognize an aspiration for internal change, he indicated that there was a significant gap to bridge between what was proposed and the behavior that continued to be demonstrated in meetings. Åslaug Marie Haga, a former diplomat and Norwegian politician, and current executive director of The Crop Trust, shares Rasmus's perspective regarding her own interactions with the UN. Command-and-control has no place in addressing the big issues that confront our societies, and she strongly believes that it is time to rethink the purpose and leadership of such multilateral bodies if they are going to meet our needs in the future.

Often new ideas, new working practices, new ways of organizing and leading, require time to take root. They have to be seeded for the benefit of future generations, only flourishing when the old guard has moved on. Alternatively, as Niclas Carlsson of the Founders Alliance suggests, these ideas take hold like a virus that has been introduced by a foreign body, gradually infecting others as they spread, adapting and mutating as they resist organizational antibodies. Open and constant communication that overcomes structural boundaries, cultural differentiation and linguistic hurdles is essential. There are a number of ways in which this can happen, with the Nordic leader facilitating the contagion from within or at the edges of the organization.

One method, as Vagn Sørensen and Sanna Suvanto-Harsaae have discovered, is to become serial board members, cross-fertilizing ideas and methods across national borders and between industries. Vagn, recalling his experiences when president and chief executive of Austrian Airlines, speaks of the cultural challenges of working in Austria where everyone else looks to you as the leader to make a decision, while Sanna acknowledges that she has encountered a similar obeisance in her work in Germany. Both recognize the need to adapt to different governance frameworks and boardroom dynamics that can be encountered in other countries. There is a need to be flexible and accept that your way is not the only way but that it can be blended with existing practices.

In Åslaug Marie's case with The Crop Trust, this blending results from taking on a senior executive role in a multinational body based in another country. The executive helps expedite change through exposing colleagues to different practices, which they model themselves and integrate with the existing culture, gradually transforming it. Exposure, guidance, inclusion and questioning all help spread the virus. This reflects what Thomas Pedersen, founder of OneLogin, has achieved with his company in the United States. He has sought to overcome the ingrained deference to hierarchy that he encountered among American colleagues, demonstrating that to question should be a two-way flow. If people do not express their point of view, how can better decisions be made?

Intriguingly, Thomas has found that when interviewing young prospects to join OneLogin, many now ask questions about values and culture. It raises an important consideration for a Nordic entrepreneur founding a new company overseas or for an established Nordic organization expanding into a foreign locale.

As Humphrey Lau of Grundfos China notes, simply to impose overseas what works in Norway or Finland or any other Nordic nation would be short-sighted, imperialist even. It is necessary, in Humphrey's view, for a company to stay true to its values and to attract local employees, business partners and customers through an alignment with their own values. If you set up in China, in other words, do not seek simply to become a Chinese company but do not remain uniquely Nordic either. Remain open to finding a middle ground where people share values and purpose regardless of where they hail from.

It is notable, in fact, how many Nordic organizations favor employing local leaders in their overseas ventures, appreciating the cultural understanding and sensitivity they bring to bear in their interaction with other people from the region. It was no coincidence that when Henrik left Navision it was an Australian that replaced him. Chris was also replaced by an Italian when he left Milan. The country managers appointed by Rasmus's department at the Danish Refugee Council are all from those same countries. Importantly, though, each one of them has bought into the leadership principles of the parent organization. The Danish Refugee Council provides principles that establish a loose framework, but it is those country managers that operate with a spirit of independence and self-reliance who will most fully benefit their local communities.

CHAPTER 10

INDUSTRIOUSNESS

He should get up early, the man who has few workers
and set about his work with thought;
much gets held up for the man sleeping in in the morning;
wealth is half-won by activity.
~ *The Poetic Edda*, Sayings of the High One, Stanza 59

There is a cultural difference here, a willingness to be
unsettled: men trapped by long winters, barely scratch-
ing a living out of narrow lands, found the sea their
obvious escape. They had no great riches to defend at
home, no neighbour enemies. They had every reason to
move on and on.
~ Michael Pye, *The Edge of the World*

In Norse mythology, the story of the Master Builder illustrates
both the deviousness of the gods and the value that Viking society placed on hard work that produced something durable

and of quality. A Viking took pride in carrying out any work to the best of their ability, providing for their family or supporting their community. The indolent lacked honor and deserved no respect. The master craftsman always strived for excellence, not only in their chosen profession but in everything they did in life, whether this was building a ship, erecting a longhouse, making weapons, growing crops or tending a flock.

In the myth of the Master Builder, the Æsir determine that they need to erect a wall around their home in Asgard to protect them from potential attack by giants and trolls. A man offers his services, undertaking to construct the wall, assisted only by his horse Svaðilfari. In return, persuaded by Loki, the gods promise him the hand of Freyja in marriage, as well as the sun and moon, on the condition that he complete his endeavor by the start of summer. Loki is convinced that it is an impossible task, with no risk of the gods having to fulfill their side of the bargain. Instead, they will have the foundations in place to complete the construction of the fortifications themselves. The unnamed builder and Svaðilfari apply themselves to their task with skill and efficiency. Their progress is swift, the wall they construct of the highest quality. Their strength, however, raises suspicions among the gods that the builder may in fact be a frost giant in disguise. Fearful of losing Freyja, as the work nears completion, they direct their ire at Loki, who is tasked with finding a solution to the problem he has been instrumental in creating. Loki shapeshifts into a mare in heat, attracting the amorous attentions of Svaðilfari, which causes the necessary delay in the builder's work and his forfeit of any claim on Freyja, the sun or moon. The story ends with the death of the enraged frost giant, now in his true form, at the hands of Thor. But the legacy of the craftsman's work endures for the gods' protection and enjoyment, at least until the cataclysm that is *Ragnarök*.

This brief account, recorded by Snorri Sturluson in *The Prose Edda*, is multilayered and highly nuanced. It includes the appreciation of craftsmanship, personal mastery and the benefits of applying ourselves to a task. Hard work can bear fruits. Industriousness is not only about meeting present need but providing for future generations. Yet the story also highlights the requirement for openness and transparency in our dealings with others, illustrating the benefits of trust in our personal relationships and business transactions. There is something too in this story about the abdication of responsibility and the detrimental effects, on the one hand, of a sense of entitlement and, on the other, of the blame game, pointing the finger at others for shortcomings and failures rather than assuming responsibility yourself.

The same issues swirl around the debate that relates to the effectiveness and durability of the welfare state system in contemporary Nordic society, especially with increased longevity of human life and the burden it places on healthcare, social care and pension schemes. One camp points to the trust engrained in Nordic culture, with tax payers having faith that governments will use their money in the right way; that they will support the aged, continue to provide education services and supply a safety net for those who, for whatever reason, find themselves without work. In the other camp are those who argue that the welfare system encourages dependency, with individuals relinquishing control while retaining an expectation that others will provide for and service their needs.

As we have seen in previous chapters, what currently prevails in Nordic society is interactive and communal, achieving a balance between giving and taking. Which is not to say that there is not a strain on the system, entangled with the big issues that confront not only Nordic nations but the global community itself, from mass migration to climate change to economic crisis. If the numbers in work diminish, but the population ages, there will come a time when the system will lose its equilibrium. Nevertheless, when queried about the characteristics that they associate with Nordic leadership, several who were interviewed for *Return of the Vikings* highlighted the entrepreneurial spirit. This is facilitated in part by having that welfare system to fall back on, but, paradoxically, is embodied by individuals who are often motivated by stretching, breaking or transforming the very status quo such a system represents.

Former Danish Prime Minister Anders Fogh Rasmussen acknowledged that Nordic leadership was exportable, especially when adapted and applied in the right context. But he also advocated for home use, arguing that it gives the Nordic nations themselves an advantage in global trade and international relations. Entrepreneurship, creativity and innovation can provide a competitive advantage when your economy is dependent less on the exploitation of natural resources or large-scale manufacturing and more on knowledge work and service provision. While there are some big brand names in Denmark that command global recognition and admiration, such as Lego, Carlsberg and Novo Nordisk, in the modern era the country has become known for how innovators and risk takers have pushed the boundaries of design, gastronomy and wind energy rather than for the production of widgets.

With freedom and autonomy comes a willingness to experiment and try things out, taking your own initiative rather than waiting to be told what to do by a superior. This is what can generate new ways of thinking, new ways of organizing, new technologies. Thomas Pedersen, co-founder and chief executive of the US-based OneLogin, suggests that the entrepreneur not only evidences a greater appetite for risk than people in traditional organizations, but also thrives on uncertainty. Not knowing is what motivates them, urging them forward in the pursuit of new knowledge, the resolution of challenges and the leveraging of unforeseen opportunities. In Thomas's view, formal education is less of a requirement than a personal inner drive and willingness to learn constantly.

Serial entrepreneur Jon Krogh epitomizes this eclectic and unconventional approach to learning. Although now resident in Greenland, his early childhood was spent in Zealand and Freetown Christiania. Jon speaks of learning from "the school of hard knocks", from experimentation, success and failure. He has been a serial founder of organizations, most recently in tourism, sometimes supplementing his own adventures with work in mainstream organizations like Tele-Post. An early crafts-related entrepreneurial foray making tabletops taught him much about quality, pricing, selling, delivery and customer interaction. He gained far more from doing than he ever would have from a book. It enabled him to apply what he had experienced under the Waldorf schooling system, which endowed him with a holistic approach to learning, integrating the theoretical, practical and artistic. In keeping with others who are possessed of an entrepreneurial mindset, what Jon does he tends to do quickly. He likes to involve others, including his customers and colleagues, in his initiatives, but with no concession to slowing down. He is always on the lookout for what is next, conscious that he is unable to focus on a single thing for too long. This is an attitude that is shared by Niclas Carlsson, founder and chief executive of the Stockholm-based Founders Alliance. Like Jon, Niclas feels the need to act, describing himself as a "mega doer". His speed of action, however, is neither aimless nor deadline-driven just for the sake of delivery. As he frames it, "The quality is the deadline." For all the action-orientation, though, the organizational culture that he nurtures is based more on principles and values than practices. Where Jon is interested in intuitive design that in some way shapes human behavior, Niclas seeks to gain understanding of other people through the social sciences and humanities, drawing on anthropology, psychology and behavioral studies.

The emphasis on speed opens up some intriguing variations between traditional enterprise and start-up business, between industry sectors and between nationalities, although with the latter there is always a danger of succumbing to stereotypes. In an essay published in the book *Nordic Ways*, Petter Stordalen, the Norwegian investor, property developer and owner of the Nordic Choice Hotels empire, focuses on taking advantage of the similarities and enjoying the complementarity of the differences. "Three words describe what we have in common. We are honest, honourable and effective. Those qualities are a competitive advantage in international terms. Also, the flat structure of Nordic companies enables us to make quick decisions, and Norwegians, Swedes, Finns and Danes work well together. The Danes say what they mean—no filter, no fuzz. The Swedes value process and a strong meeting culture, while the Norwegians are more impatient and want things done fast."

Sanna Suvanto-Harsaae has a subtler, more multifaceted perspective. A Finn based in Denmark for many years, who has also worked in Sweden, Germany and Switzerland, Sanna has enjoyed a lengthy career as a professional board member with international organizations. Currently, she is involved in the boards of Scandinavian Airlines, BabySam, the Paulig Group and the Center for Political Studies (CEPOS), among several others. She fulfills the role of Chair at numerous companies too, including BoConcept, Workz, Svane Køkkenet, Footway and Altia. Her experience is that the Nordic tendency towards conformism in big business and established enterprises, with a particular reliance on consensus, can have a dragging effect. In a business world in thrall to speed, there is a need for agility and flexibility—more speedboats, fewer oil tankers.

Do openness and inclusion create a competitive disadvantage, then, by slowing organizations down? Or, as we have already suggested, does "slow" time invested in communicating, sharing and aligning allow for a more responsive company that can react with agility once the decisions have been made? In the rush to act, how do leaders ensure that the corporate vision, principles and purpose inform what is being done; that activity is steered in the preferred direction rather than creating a mess that will take a long time to clear up? Business adviser and learning designer Kenneth Mikkelsen argues that in the current environment of complexity, too many people become stuck in action or reaction mode and fall into the "execution trap". The danger is that such action-oriented people leave little time for thinking, reflection, questioning and gaining understanding. While Sanna has experienced difficulties in large enterprises, stymied by the need to include too many people, she maintains that the Nordic leadership style lends itself well to the start-up business. Here, a small number of people by necessity perform as multidisciplinarians. They work within close proximity either in person or online, constantly sharing and testing out ideas with one another. Openness, transparency, inclusion, shared decision-making, agile development, feedback, review, learning—all these are part of the start-up's lifeblood, with everyone involved no matter their nominal role or position on the organization chart. What is fascinating, though, is what happens when such businesses begin to grow, transforming from small start-ups to medium or large enterprises. To what extent is their founder ethos maintained? Do they remain open or begin to close down, becoming more bureaucratic, more rigid, in the process? Do they retain a highly complex, networked structure, or simplify with boxes and lines, creating a more overt hierarchy in the management of space, relationships and access?

Henrik's work with mergers and acquisitions and his role with the Danish–American Chamber of Commerce has exposed him to many companies founded in the Silicon Valley region in California. The same applies to Adiba Barney through her executive roles with Silicon Vikings and the Silicon Valley Forum. Here, during the true start-up phase of these organizations, there is little to distinguish between the operation and shared values of the start-up teams in California and those in Stockholm or Helsinki or anywhere else in the Nordic region. Heini Zachariassen is founder and chief executive officer of Vivino, the world's largest digital wine community. He urges entrepreneurial companies in Silicon Valley to apply the values associated with Nordic leadership in order to keep their teams engaged and limit instability. He feels that if leaders do not share with, appreciate and include their team members, they will lose them. These are highly skilled individuals who can—and do—walk into another job in the region at a moment's notice. Heini therefore warns against a hierarchical approach to management

There is one significant caveat in all these comparisons, as consultant and business psychologist Pernille Hippe Brun highlights: what is considered cutting edge in the United States is viewed as normal in the Nordics. Community and collaboration, openness and transparency, shared learning and teamwork on projects have all become standardized in Nordic culture. This is how Nordic people were schooled, how they have always worked, how they give back to the society in which they live. It is noticeable, though, that several entrepreneurs, in a desire to adapt to a different cultural context, have sought to hybridize Nordic leadership practices with models advocated by MBA business school programs. Adiba recognizes that this has been an approach that she has adopted herself since moving from Sweden to California, striking a balance between what is familiar for her US staff and a move away from the micromanagement that she associates with many American companies.

Michael Kretz, founder and executive partner of IT consultancy firm QGroup, has followed a similar pattern. QGroup itself, which has its headquarters in Malmo, Sweden, serves as an umbrella organization. In reality, it is comprised of numerous small companies, each of which has a degree of freedom in how it operates and the culture it develops, although each company is required to subscribe to some core practices around recruitment, client interaction, delivery and administration. These are infused with Nordic leadership ideas about an inverted hierarchy, the importance of listening, learning, forgiving mistakes and even holiday allowance. Nevertheless, the emphasis the company places on recruiting established "stars" and its complex, gamified performance development system is very American in flavor. Even in Iceland, Friðrik Bjarnason's tough-love, hands-on approach to the management of Eskimos, the travel company he founded, appears as indebted to a US university education in International Relations as to the independent thinking and single-mindedness for which his fellow countrymen are known.

The role venture capitalists play in Silicon Valley soon widens the gap between a US start-up and a Nordic one. Profit is too often placed before purpose. So, in the desire to maximize profits of the new business, the venture capitalists begin to change the organizational culture that caused all the excitement in the first place. They pressure inexperienced founders to bring in seasoned professional executives to work alongside them. They in turn add structure and order, introducing new layers of bureaucracy and red tape, quantitative measures and performance assessments, business school-sanctioned practices, all of which require managerial oversight. As the organization expands, like a human in middle age, it thickens around the middle, becoming slower, a little less responsive to the customers who helped make it what it was in the first place. This is a tale that has been repeated over and over. It is certainly one that can be applied to most technology companies founded in Silicon Valley during the past two decades.

We do not wish to suggest, though, that the Nordic start-up is entirely resistant to such changes as it grows. For it too is subject to the influence of local and international investors with a strong interest in the company's success. Growth also affects the speed and agility with which organizations can act and respond, as Sanna suggests. But in the case of a Nordic company transitioning from start-up to big business, these speed issues are often related to the durability of traits such as openness and inclusion that were evident when the company was founded. These not only remain part of the organizational culture of the more established company, but they are rooted in Nordic society itself. Therefore, it inevitably takes longer to make decisions when more people have to be consulted. The fact that the leader of a large Nordic multinational, Lars Rebien Sørensen, has been recognized by *Harvard Business Review* as the world's best-performing chief executive for two years in succession, rather than the founder and leader of a vibrant US start-up or platform owner, speaks volumes about how the Nordic leadership model scales across all sizes of organization.

Business adviser and researcher Esko Kilpi has spent many years studying and advising start-ups in Europe, Asia and North America. He believes that there are lessons from both their successes and failures that can benefit the operation of any business, many of which he abstracts into regular blog posts and a recent essay collection that he edited, *Perspectives on New Work*. Esko argues that the small, agile methods practiced in the start-up environment provide a model for a post-industrial era of work. He acknowledges, however, that some of the behaviors and values that are evident in larger Nordic organizations share a lineage with what he has observed in the start-ups. Such ideas can provide a useful point of reference for established international enterprises seeking to modernize, adapting what they learn to suit their own cultural context.

In the book *The Viking Manifesto*, Steve Strid and Claes Andréasson observe, "Living in a small country can be a great advantage in today's increasingly interdependent global economy. The smaller the home market, the greater the incentive to export. Small countries often have their eyes to the world and their ears to the ground, listening for opportunities. Small countries are quicker to learn new languages, adopt new technology, faster to put aside their own mindsets in order to understand the mindsets of cultures around them." It is a point picked up by Kenneth Mikkelsen, who reflects on how the Vikings tended to move quickly, crossing seas, finding new territory, establishing trade routes. When they made new lands their own, they switched from fast to slow, from warriors and adventurers to farmers, craftsmen and tradespeople. When we settle, Kenneth argues, we can become risk-averse and protective; guarding what we have rather than seeking change. But when you have nothing—in terms of land, goods and natural resources—you have to head into the unknown. This was the impetus behind the Vikings as explorers and conquerors, taking them to the American continent, the edges of Asia and into the Mediterranean.

Petter Stordalen believes that as far as the Nordics are concerned, "In the eyes of the world, we are all Vikings", so why not take advantage of that preconception? In the modern era, Swiss-based Danish entrepreneur and investor Lars Tvede suggests, many young Nordic people share the Vikings' sense of adventure. They are proud of their national heritage while simultaneously they consider themselves global citizens. Like the Vikings, they too are daring and tolerant of risk, valuing freedom, sometimes even motivated by boredom. In his view, this outward gaze, innate creativity and willingness to make use of the time available to them, makes innovation, or at least experimentation in pursuit of it, inevitable. Esko also highlights how the survival instinct of the Vikings persists today. He argues that in the current political and economic climate, more and more Nordic companies are looking beyond the stagnant markets of Europe and the threat posed by Russia to the opportunities that can be found in China. This applies in particular to the young digital and mobile start-ups that have become integral to the Nordic economy in the current century. Digital is not just about the product or service being offered and its relevance to mobile and online markets. It is also about how these companies operate as small nodes in dispersed networks. The success of file-sharing, communication, gaming and music companies like KaZaA, Skype, Supercell, Spotify and appear.in tap into Nordic ideas about free enterprise, freedom of expression and community but they also speak to new ways of thinking about society, work, knowledge and sharing that transcend national or corporate boundaries. In Lars Tvede's view, decentralization is key to both the services they provide and their own operation. "Small units that cooperate and compete in shifting patterns tend to create amazing self-organizing complexity, spontaneous creativity and overall antifragility."

In their book *The Renaissance Society*, Rolf Jensen and Mika Aaltonen state that "the last century was about big; this century is about small". This echoes American technologist David Weinberger's web-inspired ideas that modern business and communities in a networked world are in effect "small pieces loosely joined". The hyperlink, as Weinberger and his colleagues contend in their best selling book *Cluetrain Manifesto*, is a bridge that bypasses traditional organizational hierarchies. It flattens the distance between the edge and the center. It dissolves the industrial conception of time and space. It enables swift interactions with suppliers, partners, contractors and customers. It facilitates speed to market and feedback loops that aid product refinement. In other words, everything Nordic companies have been practicing in the physical world is now happening online, regardless of the provenance of the company or location of the people involved. The Nordics were digital before *digital* was even defined. What is more, in companies like Nokia and Ericsson, both founded in the mid-nineteenth-century, the Nordics also have a long history in information and communication technology. Today, their start-ups continue to push the boundaries of what is possible in the field.

Tradeshift is one example, co-founded by Christian Lanng, Mikkel Hippe Brun and Gert Sylvest, who had previously worked together in the Danish public sector on Easytrade, an open-source trade platform. Similarly, Tradeshift is a business network, dependent on cloud-based technologies, that connects buyers and suppliers, including a free invoicing service. Its scope is broader, however, looking at the global market rather than just a European one. The company launched in 2010 and has grown rapidly, attracting investor funding from the likes of Morten Lund, Pay-Pal, Amex, Notion Capital and Scentan Ventures, reflecting the multinational nature of the business. Tradeshift supports hundreds of thousands of companies across 190 countries. These range from small-to-medium-sized businesses to large Fortune 500 enterprises, as well as public sector behemoths like the UK's National Health Service. In 2016, Tradeshift entered into a strategic partnership with Baiwang, helping to facilitate the digitization of cross-border trade and the implementation of China's internet-plus strategy intended to modernize that nation's economy.

Icelandic former politician and academic Jón Baldvin Hannibalsson argues that, during the last century, the Nordics alighted on a "third way". This shies away from the failed neoliberalist capitalism of the United States that has resulted in frequent economic instability and from the totalitarianism of Soviet Communism. It achieves a compromise between the extremes of the ideologies that had such an impact from World War I onwards. The Nordics have accepted enterprise and a market system but with greater limitations, including strict regulation by a democratic state. As we have observed, the risk undertaken by the entrepreneur is leavened by the protection provided by the welfare state should the endeavor fail. In recent years, we have witnessed how digital and mobile technology have enabled trans-national communal action as people have come together to counter totalitarian regimes and economic models that are unfit for the long term, benefitting only a tiny minority of people. Do digital and mobile technology have the potential to take this third way into the global mainstream?

What Nordic businesses, large and small, tend to demonstrate are high levels of responsiveness. Their open cultures mean that they are generally able to resist the rigidity and ossification that can affect ageing or expanding organizations. In the mobile technology, app development and computer software industries, all of which are prominent in the Nordics, there is a cycle of development and testing that often involves representatives from the target users of these products and services. This can go through many iterations, with the penultimate known as Beta testing. Canadian consultant Harold Jarche contends that in the era of digital networks, in order to remain relevant and responsive, we have to maintain a state of "perpetual Beta".

This requires being open not only internally but externally too, adapting to and accommodating outside influences. The Novozymes research project featured in the documentary *Collaboration* by Katja Gry Birkegaard Carlsen and Alfred Birkegaard Hansted is a good example of this, where a competitive edge is relinquished in pursuit of a greater good. This research-and-development initiative sought to connect with a global scientific community, enabling international collaboration and co-creation of solutions. The project sought to leverage the networking opportunities enabled by social media, bringing together bio-innovators wherever they happened to be, facilitating the exchange of ideas and the sharing of findings. The project's focus, therefore, was on innovation, connection and communication. It positioned Novozymes as an innovation partner servicing a global scientific community. It is collective industriousness intended to address the needs of future generations.

CHAPTER 11

PERSEVERANCE

Night is eagerly awaited by him who can rely on his
provisions;
short are a ship's yards,
changeable are autumn nights,
many kinds of weathers in five days,
and more in one month.
~ *The Poetic Edda*, Sayings of the High One, Stanza 74

In sum, no matter the domain, the highly successful
had a kind of ferocious determination that played out in
two ways. First, these exemplars were unusually resil-
ient and hardworking. Second, they knew in a very, very
deep way what it was they wanted. They not only had
determination, they had *direction*.
~ Angela Duckworth, *Grit*

"It is the struggle that makes us grow," states economist, philosopher and futurist Lene Rachel Andersen. "We need to be challenged at the right level of complexity and pain. If it is too easy, people do not change. If it is too hard, they give up." This is an attitude that energy entrepreneur Mika Anttonen would recognize. His parents divorced when he was very young. At the time, this was a rare occurrence in Finland, and the subsequent belittling he experienced at the hands of a school teacher, who expressed low expectations of him because he came from a broken home, spurred him on to prove himself. It was an early life lesson, as was his father's disastrous business adventures when he went into partnership with a friend. It taught him much about endurance and fortitude, about striving to be better each day.

The Viking virtue of perseverance captures this notion of recovering from setbacks, learning from what went wrong, never giving up and accepting your place in the natural order, where the environment—the turbulence created by wind, ice, volcanic fire, stormy seas and earthquakes—can always overpower you. All the interviewees for this book were asked what the Viking heritage meant to them. Anders Fogh Rasmussen immediately highlighted the Viking quality of perseverance in the pursuit and completion of their goals, while also celebrating their adventurous quest for new frontiers, moving constantly outwards from Scandinavia, to Iceland, to Greenland, to the American continent. Kenneth Mikkelsen also valued the Vikings' responsiveness and their survival imperative that helped them adapt to the climactic and environmental conditions on land and at sea.

Adaptiveness is at the core of this ancient notion of perseverance and its ongoing relevance in contemporary society. In his book *Do Design*, business adviser Alan Moore argues that adaptiveness "is based upon a continuous process of creating, collaborating, communicating and critiquing". Such a definition serves as a useful summary for the manner in which historic Vikings explored and settled new territories, integrating with the indigenous populations where they found them in Britain, Ireland and France, as well as the day-to-day operation of a modern Nordic organization. There is also a thread here about persistence and adaptiveness that runs through Nordic society and the culture it produces.

Setbacks, learning, communication and subsequent progress are the narrative engines that drive political dramas and crime series like *Borgen*, *Forbrydelsen* (*The Killing*) and *Bron/Broen* (*The Bridge*), which have been such popular television successes at home and abroad. Birgitte Nyborg (Sidse Babett Knudsen) persists in the face of adversity no matter what her political adversaries or the media throw at her, no matter the complexities of her life at home. Sarah Lund (Sofie Gråbøl) and Saga Norén (Sofia Helin) continue relentlessly on, jumping hurdles, negotiating labyrinthine leads and dead ends, until they catch the perpetrators of the crimes they investigate. There are also gentler, more prosaic explorations of the difficulties everyday people face, including the numerous rites of passage of personal growth and relationships, from the navel-gazing minutiae of Karl Ove Knausgaard's *Min kamp* (*My Struggle*) books to Lasse Hallström's 1985 coming-of-age film *Mitt liv som hund* (*My Life as a Dog*), adapted from a novel by Reidar Jönsson.

My Life as a Dog is a gentle comedy set in the late 1950s that celebrates human eccentricity and community. Its protagonist, the twelve-year-old Ingemar (Anton Glanzelius), stumbles from one misadventure to another, discovering ways to bounce back from mishaps and personal tragedies, to persevere with a smile eventually reappearing on his face. Unruly and accident-prone,

Ingemar proves too much for his terminally-ill mother (Anki Lidén) to cope with. He is separated from his pet dog, Sickan, and dispatched for the summer to live in a small settlement in Småland with his uncle Gunnar (Tomas von Brömssen) and aunt Ulla (Kicki Rundgren). His is a philosophical outlook. Whatever misfortune befalls him—bullying, his father's absence, his mother's illness, homesickness, separation from his pet, tempestuous friendships—are all contextualized in relation to the fate of Laika, the first dog in space, which eventually starved to death. His own doggedness is expressed frequently when he drops to his knees and barks at those around him.

Ingemar is quickly accepted into the community in Småland. He joins the local soccer team, where he befriends the green-haired Manne (Jan-Philip Hollström) and the tomboy pugilist Saga (Melinda Kinnaman). He works with his uncle on the construction of a summerhouse, frequently joining him at the glass foundry where he is employed. He chaperones another glass worker, Berit (Ing-Marie Carlsson), while she poses nude for a local sculptor. He also secretly reads from a lingerie catalog to Arvidsson (Didrik Gustavsson), who occupies the rooms below his aunt and uncle's dwelling. Or he observes the obsessional roof repairs carried out by Fransson (Magus Rask), who lives in an adjacent property. Eventually, though, Ingemar returns home where his reunion with mother and brother is all too brief.

His mother's hospitalization and subsequent death from tuberculosis find Ingemar displaced from his home once again. This time in the depths of winter, he returns to Småland, where the disappointments and setbacks accumulate until he has a cathartic breakdown. Arriving back at his aunt and uncle's home, he discovers that Arvidsson has also died, his old rooms now home to a large Greek family. The pressure on space in the building means there is no room for him at the house, and he is required to sleep where the Widow Arvidsson (Vivi Johansson) now lives. School offers little succor, further complicating his relationship with Saga, which treads a thin line between close friendship and amorousness. Jealousy of Ingemar's friendship with another girl prompts Saga to reveal that his beloved dog has been put down rather than housed in kennels, and then to apply a beating in the makeshift boxing ring they use.

Ingemar takes refuge in his uncle's summerhouse. Here he processes the loss of parent and beloved pet. He reflects on what he perceives as his rejection and the rootlessness it has caused, as he has been shifted from one house to another, from parents to carers to relatives. He considers the effects of friendship and love for another human. Everything he observes through the lens of Laika's misfortune in space. By the morning, after a difficult night, he is ready to rejoin friends and family, all of whom have been drawn together again by the antics of Fransson who has chosen this day to go swimming in the wintry waters. By the film's end, Ingemar is once again enjoying the summer pleasures of the previous year, more comfortable with his relationship with Saga, at home in the local community. The seasons have changed, the light has returned, what was broken has been restored, and new life has followed death. Nature's rhythms subsume human comedy and tragedy alike.

Friðrik Bjarnason sees continuity between his own experiences growing up and living in Iceland and those of his Viking ancestors. Iceland is a place of extremes—between light and darkness, between winter and summer—and harsh climactic conditions, characterized by strong easterly winds and challenging seas. In such an environment, self-sufficiency achieved through farming and fishing has always been important for Icelanders. To live on the island, it is necessary constantly to adapt to the moment. In fact, in Friðrik's view it is difficult, sometimes futile, to plan in any great depth. Icelanders are *always* living in times of extreme change. This is part and parcel of the travel industry that Friðrik is involved in through his business Eskimos. Nature has a way of reminding you of your place and disrupting human activities, as was the case when Eyjafjallajökull erupted in 2010.

In a pattern that is becoming common as more people move into metropolitan areas, Friðrik's parents both came from small towns in Iceland but met in Reykavík, where he grew up before heading overseas to study. Friðrik had already been exposed to the contrasting worldviews of rural relatives and city folk. Now he sought an outsider's perspective. Birgitta Jónsdóttir has also had a peripatetic life, as we learned in chapter 4, which has resulted in global wandering and a return to her home country. While this exposure to other cultures and connection to numerous international communities has given her access to a wealth of knowledge and ideas, it has also allowed her to maintain an outsider's status in her own country. Her career as poet, artist, activist and, more recently, as politician, has been shaped by her desire to challenge from within, as well as by her courage and resilience in the face of adversity.

Birgitta's father left her mother, the folk singer Bergþóra Árnadóttir, when she was still an infant. After her mother's remarriage, she grew up in a small community of the type Friðrik's parents had left behind, where her adoptive father, Jón Ólafsson, was a fisherman. In 1987, when Birgitta was twenty years of age, he committed suicide by walking into a river during a storm. Subsequently, Birgitta's first husband, Charles Egill Hirt, who suffered from epilepsy, went missing in 1993 and his body was not discovered for another five years. She describes how, during this period of not knowing and raising their child as a single mother, she learned how to live and cope in a situation of extreme uncertainty, which helped her later in life to deal with complex and difficult circumstances. As she rose to prominence during the financial crisis and entered Icelandic politics, she was able to draw on experiences and strengths developed during a time of personal family tragedy.

In interviews, her own writing and public talks, Birgitta speaks of passion, purpose, hope and perseverance. All are key ingredients in what psychologist Angela Duckworth defines as *grit*, which she describes as "having a passion to accomplish a particular top-level goal and the perseverance to follow through". Like Mika, Birgitta acquired the grit-like practice of trying to make each day better than the last, and she set her sights on realizing big visions. In Mika's case, they consist in a sustainable and environmentally-friendly solution to our energy provision and storage. In Birgitta's, a radical overhaul of the socio-political system in Iceland and, on the global stage, the promotion of and adherence to fundamental human rights, particularly as they relate to freedom of expression, freedom of information and protection of personal data.

In her study of grit, Duckworth makes the connection between her own ideas and the Finnish concept of sisu, which we encountered briefly at the close of chapter 3. This encapsulates the notion of finishing what you start, never quitting in the middle of something, refraining from whining about your lot in life, demonstrating resilience, determination and perseverance in the face of failure. It captures the stoicism of the Finnish people. But also reflects their history and ability to adapt and endure. The nation we now know as Finland, as we briefly explored in chapter 9, has served as a pawn and battleground in historic struggles between Sweden and Russia, as well as the site of a bloody civil war early in the twentieth-century. Such experiences have helped forge a national identity of which sisu is a part. In an interview, Supercell chief executive Ilkka Paananen contextualizes sisu as "a national characteristic, a kind of patriotic self-identification like the 'British Bulldog spirit' or the 'American Dream'". He believes that sisu, the inner fire that it grants the individual, goes a long way to explaining the success of many Finnish start-ups.

The filmmaker Aki Kaurismäki has made an art form out of grittiness, infusing his works with its spirit. Kaurismäki's filmography is filled with offbeat comedies and melodramas about people who persevere despite the odds. Against the backdrop of a major economic depression that affected the northern, more industrialized region of Finland in the early-to-mid 1990s, Kaurismäki created what is known as his "Loser Trilogy". The first installment, *Kauas pilvet karkaavat* (*Drifting Clouds*), which was released in 1996, is an overt tribute to the *sisu* of the Finnish people. It follows the struggles of a middle-aged couple, Lauri (Kari Väänänen) and Ilona (Kati Outinen), as the recession begins to bite. Their bereavement through the loss of their young child is subtly indicated, although this has occurred long before the film's events, which focus largely on issues relating to employment and indebtedness.

Lauri is a tram driver on the Helsinki network and Ilona is head of the waiting staff at the *Dubrovnik* restaurant. They live in a small apartment, the living room of which is mostly furnished with items purchased on credit, including a sofa, bookcase and television. When the tram operator decides to downsize, the boss requests that each driver pick a card from a playing deck. The three with the cards of least value lose their jobs, with Lauri among their number. Too proud to "live off the state", Lauri is instead dependent on Ilona's income to service their debts and support them while he seeks a new role. He soon learns that his age counts against him, and he begins to seek solace in alcohol. When he fails a medical for a potential job as a bus driver because of a previously undetected hearing disability, he loses his license, closing off one avenue back to employment.

Meanwhile, Ilona has largely been responsible for the smooth operation of the *Dubrovnik* restaurant. On behalf of the owner, Mrs. Sjöholm (Elina Salo), she manages the customer interactions and maintains order in the kitchen, where the head chef Lajunen (Markku Peltola) occasionally succumbs to the temptations of the bottle. The day after Lauri's final shift at the tram company, she discovers that *Dubrovnik* is to be sold to a restaurant chain, in part to pay off Mrs. Sjöholm's own debts. She too is now without work and confronted with age and gender prejudices. One short-lived job at a run-down bar sees her at her efficient best. But her good will is exploited by its owner, a small-time criminal, who not only fails to pay Ilona but gets her into trouble with the tax authorities. He and his companions administer a severe beating to Lauri when he tries to collect what money is owed to her.

As their apartment is silently emptied of items they can no longer afford to pay for, Lauri makes a little money by selling his imported American car. The couple opt to gamble the proceeds in the hope of increasing their meagre nest egg, but instead lose it all. Throughout this period, Ilona has intermittent encounters with the former *Dubrovnik* doorman, Melartin (Sakari Kuosmanen), which often descend into heavy drinking, a temporary release from the challenges that face them. It is Melartin, however, that plants the idea that ultimately changes their fortunes. He convinces Ilona that it is she, with all her knowledge of the business, who should open her own restaurant. Lauri, too, is persuaded by the idea and supports Ilona as she develops a business plan for the scheme. Without any capital, however, their bank is reluctant to back the venture. It is a chance encounter with the retired and restless Mrs. Sjöholm that makes the new restaurant idea viable. She is willing to back Ilona, providing funds that can be repaid once the new business is firmly established. Ilona, Lauri and Melartin reassemble the old *Dubrovnik* team, including Lajunen, whom they find among the homeless and transport to a sanatorium to wean him off his alcohol dependency. They unite under a restaurant name that signals their purpose and desire: *Ravintola työ*, which translates as *Restaurant Work*.

The film closes on the new restaurant's opening day. Ilona, Lauri and Mrs. Sjöholm look on nervously as the minutes tick by through the lunch hour with no patrons coming through the door. But by mid-afternoon, everything has changed. The restaurant is packed and Lauri has just accepted an evening booking for thirty people. The couple take a moment away from the busy scene, staring at the drifting clouds, reflecting on their own grit and resilience, as well as the mutual trust and support of the small community that now surrounds them. *Drifting Clouds* is a celebration of perseverance. It shows how a combination of personal will, luck, and all the virtues, from courage to industriousness, can help transform challenges and difficulties into opportunities. Sometimes, though, people desist, unable to continue with the struggle, worn down by opposition and resistance.

Interviewed for *Return of the Vikings*, Jørgen Lindegaard, former president and chief executive of Scandinavian Airlines, expressed his regret that he had not been more persistent with one of the projects he oversaw while with the organization. This related to the creation of a low-cost airline called Snowflake as a subsidiary organization within the SAS Group, which was intended to compete with the likes of Ryanair and EasyJet.

Snowflake proved to be a fleeting addition to the airline industry. It commenced operations in March 2003 and was shuttered in October 2004. At the time, SAS was restructuring, which prompted unrest among staff and unions, resulting in industrial action. The new airline was never able to achieve the intended cost savings, as it was entirely dependent on existing SAS crews and protocols, but made use of a very small fleet. It failed, therefore, to make a profit during its short period of operation. Jørgen maintains that Snowflake was a visionary initiative that lacked success because of the unwillingness of others within SAS, particularly pilots, to cooperate. He points to the success of the low-budget Norwegian Air Shuttle business as an illustration of the viability of the project. His inference is that an idea can endure, can find a legacy, even if an individual does not persevere in their pursuit of it.

Legacy thinking is an important aspect of perseverance. From a big-picture perspective, it is connected to notions of survival and serving the needs of future generations. It is why so much effort is invested in addressing the big issues that have emerged in a world significantly transformed by industrialization. The effects of climate change have prompted Mika and many others to seek out innovative solutions to energy generation and storage, reforestation and desertification. Water safety and provision has also emerged as a serious problem to be tackled. But there are also considerations relating to migration and displacement as a result of conflict or the inhospitality of previously inhabited lands. With people increasingly drawn to metropolitan areas, there are questions to be answered regarding housing and transportation.

As human activity serves to deplete our natural resources and threaten the survival of many plant and animal species, there is also a considerable threat to food sources and their diversity.

Food security and the safeguarding of biodiversity is the mission of The Crop Trust, of which Åslaug Marie Haga is the executive director. Åslaug Marie spent her childhood on a farm in Norway, where her family grew cabbages. She has come full circle, back to crops. Originally, she intended to be a marine biologist but a study exchange in Delaware shifted her focus. Instead, she concentrated on the social sciences and then joined the foreign service for twelve years before enjoying a high-profile career in Norwegian politics. The role at The Crop Trust takes her back to her roots but also connects her to a grander purpose that relates to the longevity not only of plant species but of humanity itself.

The Crop Trust provides financial support to international gene banks established to maintain the ongoing diversity of the world's most important food crops. The Trust also assists with the efficient management of these gene banks, coordinating a global network of institutions that ensures the preservation, accessibility and use of these diverse crops. It is also responsible for the operation of the Svalbard Global Seed Vault, which has been built inside a mountain on a remote island between mainland Norway and the North Pole. The vault serves as a fail-safe backup to the various gene banks located around the globe. It is designed to store as wide a range of crop genetic material as possible against natural or man-made disaster. The vault has the capacity to store material for 4.5 million varieties of crop, holding 500 seeds for each crop type. To enable the financial security of agricultural diversity, a self-sufficient global system and the long-term maintenance of the vault, The Crop Trust has established an endowment fund intended to raise $850 million.

In addition to the conservation and fundraising work that Åslaug Marie and her colleagues are involved in, much time and effort are also allocated to education and raising awareness. The combined effects of birth rate and longevity of human life enabled by improved healthcare means that there will be an additional two billion people to feed by 2050. The situation is further complicated by rising temperatures. In fact, melted ice water found in the tunnels leading to the Svalbard Vault in early 2017 itself usefully advertised this problem, while posing no threat to the contents of the genetic material stored in the vault. It is estimated that an increase of a single degree in global temperatures can equate to a two percent reduction in agricultural yield. The loss increases exponentially as the temperature rises. Some of the varieties of crop that we are currently dependent on face a very real threat of extinction.

Humans rely on three principle crops as a source of calories. These are wheat, rice and maize. Over time, through biodiversification and experimentation, we have found ways of making different strains of these crops grow in a variety of locations and landscapes all over the world, adapting to an array of soil types, exposure to the elements and countless species of insect. But our dependency on certain chemicals to grow and protect these crops have proved harmful to the surrounding ecosystems. Our farming techniques and the problems posed by the excessive use of water and of pesticides have to be addressed, in addition to the preservation of crop seeds, if our agriculture is to remain sustainable.

Biodiversity has also enabled the richness of the human diet and that of the animals we raise as another source of nutrition. However, population increases and the impact of urbanization place a premium on the fields available to grow foodstuffs and steward animals. With certain crops no longer in the ground, it is essential that their genetic material is preserved. It may be the source of more robust crops able to withstand changing climactic and environmental conditions in the future. Or it may be hybridized with other genetic material to create the foodstuffs of the next generations, ones that can withstand temperature increases and diminishing fresh-water supplies.

For some, the Svalbard Global Seed Vault has become one of the most important buildings in the world. Its custodians, like so many of the individuals we have met during the course of researching this book, are motivated by a higher purpose. While fund-raising is essential to the mission of The Crop Trust, the organization is not one that is dependent on turning a profit or delivering shareholder return. Their responsibility is that of the good ancestor, taking into account future generations, the environment and sustainability in the decisions they make and the actions they take. But it is also about being a good descendant too, learning from and building on what went before, avoiding the repetition of mistakes, enhancing the advances and innovations, ensuring a continuity in the history and progression of humanity. One in which their own species and those on which it is interdependent endure. It is a story of survival and perseverance, of getting through the long winter and assembling supplies in the summer, just like their Viking forebears.

PART III
UNCERTAINTY

CHAPTER 12
TIMES OF EXTREME CHANGE

May he benefit, he who learnt it,
luck to those who listened!
~ *The Poetic Edda*, Sayings of the High One, Stanza 164

On the open sea there are no landmarks, there is only an amorphous, chaotic shifting of directionless masses of water that loom up and break and roll, and their surface is, in turn, broken by subsystems that interfere and form whirlpools and appear and disappear and finally vanish without a trace. Slowly this confusion will work its way into the labyrinth of my ear and dissolve my sense of orientation; it will fight its way into my cells and displace their salt concentrations and the conductive power of my nervous system as well, leaving me deaf, blind, and helpless. I'm not afraid of the sea merely because it wants to strangle me. I'm afraid of it because it will take away from me my orientation, the

inner gyroscope of my life, my awareness of what is up
and down, my connection to Absolute Space.
~ Peter Høeg, *Smilla's Sense of Snow*

Not long after the turn of the present century, when Chris's son
was ten years of age, his father used to watch him absorbed in
the mass multiplayer online role-playing game *World of Warcraft*.
This immensely popular game centers on complex and challenging quests, with players usually forming guilds comprised
of diverse groups of individuals with complementary skills and
roles. Chris observed his Danish–American son communicating
in English with people he had never met before from all around
the world. Together, they agreed strategies and developed plans
to achieve their common objectives. Their missions gave them
a shared sense of purpose. The successful accomplishment of
goals required adaptiveness and collaboration, not to mention
the high levels of trust such interdependent action entailed. This
was shared endeavor that had a social dimension to it.

Collaboration, mutual coaching, knowledge sharing and a collective approach to problem-solving is familiar to any young
person like Chris's son who has grown up in a Nordic country.
These qualities are characteristic of their school experiences, social interactions and leisure activities. They are not confined to
online communities but inform their expectations and desires
about the world they live in and how they now approach work.
For them, it is natural that they should have access to leadership and guidance, that they can voice their own opinions and
influence decision-making, that they will experience personal
autonomy in service of the collective, that leadership will be values-based and purposeful. There is nothing utopian or idealistic
about this. It is how they have always tackled issues or taken
advantage of opportunities.

Such a participatory and connective mindset is essential in navigating times of extreme change. It enables greater fluidity and responsiveness. To paraphrase network analyst Valdis Krebs, such people connect on their similarities and benefit from their differences. They cohere into small communities that form in response to a specific set of circumstances and needs, work together and then disband as the context changes. This occurs in an ever-shifting network in which knowledge, leadership and accountability is in free flow rather than resident in a particular location or with a single individual. It represents a way of organizing that transcends traditional considerations of status, job title and expertise. It also ignores divisions and boundaries suggested by notions of corporate structure or even national borders. Their outlook is global rather than insular, their long reach facilitated by a digital infrastructure that supplements what they can do in the physical domain.

In her book *Frantumaglia*, Elena Ferrante writes, "Borders make us feel stable. At the first hint of conflict, at the least threat, we close them. The border serves to gather us into a unit, to diminish the hidden centrifugal thrusts that undermine our identity. But it's purely an appearance. A story begins when, one after another, our borders collapse." For all the retrenchment signalled by Brexit in the United Kingdom and the election of Donald Trump in the United States, there is an increasing sense of uncertainty and ambiguity regarding how we understand and relate to the world. Our frames of reference, from national borders to a sense of self, are in question. What seemed factual and inviolable yesterday is cast into doubt today, then disproven tomorrow. Our acquisition of new knowledge, the latest scientific discoveries, makes it seem that our intellectual foundations rest on dunes of moving sand. The certainty and knowledge bequeathed us by the Renaissance and the Enlightenment has become hazier with each passing year.

Phycisist and astronomer Marcelo Gleiser argues that we can consider all our accumulated knowledge as an island. That island has grown with the passage of time as we have learned more about our world and the cosmos that surrounds it. However, as the island has grown, so has its coastline, which borders the ocean of the unknown. The more we know, in other words, the more there is still to be known. Our certainties are counterbalanced by uncertainties, our facts by ambiguities. With their innovative mixture of sail and oar, and boats that could traverse both sea and river, the Vikings sought to explore the waters of the unknown, adding to existing knowledge, discovering and guiding others to new territories. They combined curiosity, technical virtuosity and leadership in navigating their own times of tumult and change. These attributes persist in their Nordic descendants who provide an example of how to negotiate contemporary complexities.

Every generation appears to believe that it is living through times of extreme change. That is part of the human condition, reflected in the history of movement, settlement, ideas, technology, communication and warfare. It is evident in the transitions from nomadism to agricultural communities to city states to nationhood. Or the spread of knowledge and stories that evolved from an oral tradition to written manuscripts to mass printing to the dissemination of electronic text, photographs and moving images on mobile devices. "Chaos is a kind of gravity," according to the narrator of Karl Ove Knausgaard's Min kamp (My Struggle) books, "and the rhythm you can sense in history, of the rise and fall of civilizations, is perhaps caused by this. It is remarkable that the extremes resemble each other, in one sense at any rate, for in both immense chaos and in a strictly regulated, demarcated world the individual is nothing, life is everything." Frequently, we find ourselves negotiating the continuum between these two extremes.

Over the past few decades, however, there is a conception that everything has accelerated as we have witnessed the swing away from manual to knowledge work, the sweeping effects of digitization and the growing self-knowledge that accompanies scientific progress. The pace of life, the rate of change, the nature of business, all appear increasingly frenetic. A sense of urgency also has been created as we have become more aware of the effects of human behavior and action on our environment. Industrialization, urbanization, population growth, advances in healthcare, longevity of life, agricultural practice, the burning of fossil fuels, military conflict, transportation and global mass migration all affect the delicate ecosystem that supports us. Each of these poses a significant issue that remains to be addressed as we advance through the current century and prepare the way for future generations.

In the wake of the Cold War, during which the enemy was known and understood, the US Army War College adopted the acronym VUCA. This was used to describe the volatility, uncertainty, complexity and ambiguity that characterized a new form of conflict, often with unknown insurgents or terrorists, that increasingly leaked from the physical world into the digital one. The military's search for methods with which to accommodate and adapt to this new landscape soon became relevant to the socio-political and business domains too. The instability and unrest extends beyond warfare. It is apparent in issues relating to climate change, social inequality, the uneven distribution of wealth, migration, economic crisis, energy generation, sustainable food sources, water security, biological technologies, automation, artificial intelligence and employment.

In a world that can no longer offer lifetime jobs, and is already seeing the historic employer–employee arrangement fragmented by the gig economy, what will the future model be? In a post-industrial age, will we have a jobless society? Could the Nordic nations, with their established welfare state system and charitable service of community, be better equipped to adapt than those societies that champion the self-made individual? Or will the burden placed on the already over-strained public services finally break them? Could the entrepreneurial mindset hold sway? Will people place emphasis on creating their own jobs, circumventing established social and corporate infrastructures? What might be the alternative methods of value exchange? Will we witness an increase in the gift economy or in bartering?

The behaviors already modeled by the *World of Warcraft* generation suggest that the status quo of top-down hierarchical management systems established in the industrial era is no longer viable. The pace and scale of technological change has enabled cross-organizational, trans-national interaction. This poses a challenge to current management practices and organizational structures because it makes it possible for them to be bypassed. It also serves to collapse traditional notions of time and space regarding when and where work can be done. When you are working on a project with partners dispersed around the globe, how can a working time directive apply? If the notion of the traditional company is likely to be atomized—as a small, core organization enters into short-lived partnership with other businesses, freelancers, consultants, customers and suppliers—then so too will the working day and traditional ideas regarding what constitutes a workplace.

All of which points to the need for a responsive style of leadership that can provide vision and direction rather than a manager who simply monitors and quantifies. This is leadership among equals. The servant who facilitates. The individual who steps aside when the context requires it, taking direction from those more knowledgeable and experienced regarding the matter in hand. The communicator who helps people see the big picture and their place in it, using stories to convey mission, values, objectives and learning. The navigator who helps steer through the blizzard storm, deriving some form of sense from the white noise that surrounds them. The aesthete who brings simplicity and minimalism to organizational design and function.

Figures like Jan Carlzon, Åslaug Marie Haga, Claus Meyer, Birgitta Jónsdóttir and Mika Anttonen demonstrate through their personal experiences that the ability to see with your heart, nurture a values-based culture and develop trusting relationships can help pull people together into strong communities equipped and ready to serve a greater purpose. That they are able to achieve this says much about their own humility and authenticity. Not only do they make themselves accessible to their colleagues and customers, they actively seek out what others think, listen to them closely and ensure that they influence decision-making. They enable ownership and accountability among their teams, working and learning collaboratively with them.

A story from the Frankish annals illustrates this aspect of the Viking culture. When a band of Danish raiders arrived in Frankish lands, they were met by an emissary who asked to be taken to the leader of the Viking band. He was told, "We are all leaders here."

As any Viking knew when they boarded ship, for all their personal integrity, courage and honor, their success depended on those around them. To traverse the seas, or to win in battle, or to have the provisions to survive the winter required collaborative effort and an investment of trust in your companions. The virtues that informed how they lived and worked were codified, passed down to subsequent generations through both their genes and literature. It is not only the individual who perseveres, as we saw in chapter 11, but also an approach to life handed down by the Vikings that accommodates and adapts to the world's complexities. This remains part of the fabric of Nordic societies and how their organizations work.

The inclusive, trusting, collaborative style of Nordic leadership offers an alternative way to negotiate through our current times of extreme change. What many of us are now experiencing online in distributed, fluid, networked communities, the Nordics have been practicing on land and sea for centuries. While many are still developing and broadcasting their theories about the future of work, the Nordics are not waiting around to find out when the future begins. They are already leading the way. The rest of us would do well to follow their guiding northern lights.

ABOUT THE INTERVIEWEES

 **Adiba Barney** is the CEO of SVForum—Silicon Valley's largest and oldest non-profit organization, dedicated to educating and creating relationships within the technology and start-up community. She has also been the Executive Director of Silicon Vikings, a non-profit business networking organization connecting the Nordics' innovation and start-up ecosystem to Silicon Valley. Adiba was born in Lebanon but fled with her family to Sweden at age seven to escape the war. Adiba holds a BA in International Marketing and Business from Mälardalen University in Sweden and has studied Branding, PR, Media and Communication at Berghs School of Communication in Stockholm, Sweden.

Ally Jiang is an international HR professional, specializing in leadership development talent management and employee engagement. She has worked in fast-moving consumer goods and investment banking in international corporations in Europe and Asia, including MARS, Mead Johnson Nutrition, Carlsberg Breweries, Saxo Bank and Swire Group. Working in the Nordics and Asia, she is especially interested in leadership styles from different cultures and current best practices.

Anders Fogh Rasmussen has been at the center of European and global politics for over three decades as Secretary General of NATO (2009-14), Prime Minister of Denmark (2001-09), Danish Minister of Economic Affairs, and as a leading Danish parliamentarian, entering parliament at the age of 25. As Secretary General of NATO, he developed a strategic concept which sets the Alliance's core priorities for the future. In response to Russia's aggression against Ukraine, he initiated a "Readiness Action Plan". In 2014 he established the political consultancy and business advisory firm *Rasmussen Global* and in June 2016 he was appointed advisor to the President of Ukraine, Petro Poroshenko.

Annelise Goldstein is an organizational psychologist and expert in leadership, talent development and diversity. She was born and raised in the US and has been living and working in Denmark for the past 21 years. Before moving to Denmark, she worked in her early career as a researcher at the University of Pennsylvania where she became fascinated by psychoanalytic theory as a way to understand organizational life. After moving to Denmark, Annelise took the leap into "theory in practice" by holding various Human Resource specialist and leadership positions in both Novo Nordisk and most recently Nordea Bank where she worked with cultural transformation.

 **Birgitta Jónsdóttir** is a poetician and activist who served as a member of the Icelandic parliament from 2013 to 2017, representing the Pirate Party. She has helped establish two political movements that successfully landed representatives in the Icelandic parliament, The Civic Movement in 2009 and in 2013 the Pirate Party. Both political movements were elected to bring forward democratic reform, transparency and human rights in the digital era. Birgitta specializes in 21st century policy and lawmaking. The Pirate Party is currently the second/third largest party in Iceland.

 **Carmen Sanz** is a Spanish lawyer specializing in international, corporate and Norwegian maritime law. She is President of the Spanish/Norwegian Chamber of Commerce. In 2014 she was awarded Saint Olaf's medal as Knight in the First Degree in the Royal Norwegian House.

Claus Meyer has been a gastronomic entrepreneur for more than 30 years. Besides his countless companies employing more than 800 staff, Claus is an affiliated professor and distinguished alumnus at Copenhagen Business School and Social Impact Fellow at University of California Berkley Haas School of Business. Claus is a Knight of the Order under The Royal Danish House, member of the Danish Gastronomical Academy and he has been named on EAT Foundation and the Culinary Institute of America's Plant Forward Global 50.

Esko Kilpi is the Managing Director and founder of a research and consultancy firm working with the challenges of internet-based business models, digital work and sociology of value creation based in Finland. As an international speaker, author and knowledge work expert he advises both public sector organizations and leading multinational companies. Esko has been a member of the advisory board for the World Bank on knowledge management. Further, he has been a member of an expert think tank on knowledge management for the EU. Currently, he serves as an advisory board member for a select group of high tech start-ups.

Even Bratberg has held numerous senior positions within the horticultural industry, research and administration, in Norway and internationally. He was national adviser on horticulture in Norway and has been involved in the conservation and use of genetic resources for food and agriculture. Even has published a number of articles on horticultural issues and holds a MSc in Horticultural Science from Norwegian University of Life Sciences (NMBU).

Friðrik Bjarnason is the Managing Director of Eskimos, a group of travel companies based in Reykjavik, Iceland. Educated in the US, he graduated with a degree in International Relations from University of Minnesota. Fridrik started his career working in the automobile, advertising and telecommunications industries before starting his travel service company in 1999, which has since then diversified and expanded into various fields of tourism.

Heini Zachariassen is the founder and CEO of Vivino, the world's largest wine community. With more than $37 million in funding, Heini continues to drive Vivino's global expansion. Having co-founded several start-ups, including global internet and mobile security company BullGuard, he has a storied background in software development and mobile innovation and a track record for building successful global businesses. Heini leads the team from Vivino's headquarters in San Francisco, where he resides with his wife and three children.

Humphrey Lau is Group Senior Vice President and China CEO of Grundfos. He worked for more than 15 years in Novo Nordisk and was their first CEO in China. Humphrey was born in Hong Kong, raised in Denmark and lived in China for many years. He has written an acclaimed book on business in China entitled *Slå den røde dronning* ("Beat the Red Queen"). Humphrey holds an MSc in Civil Engineering from the Technical University of Denmark and a BSc in Business Administration & Economics from Copenhagen Business School.

Jan Carlzon has for decades been celebrated as a visionary leader, emphasizing the importance of the customer-driven and employee-empowered company before anyone else. He was the CEO of Scandinavian Airlines for 13 years, where he helped the company make a remarkable turnaround. Jan Carlzon's philosophy of the "customer-driven, loving, strategic leadership", first introduced in his global bestselling book *Moments of Truth* (1985), has been translated into 22 languages and continues to be more relevant now than ever. Jan Carlzon holds honorary doctorates at Pepperdine University, Los Angeles, and Pacific Lutheran University, Tacoma.

Jan Olaf Mirko Härter is a German physicist who researches a wide range of topics with focus on complex biosystems. He received his PhD in Theoretical Physics from the University of California at Santa Cruz, USA, in 2007. He then transitioned to the Max Planck Institute for Meteorology, Hamburg, Germany, where he researched climate change and extreme precipitation. Since 2011 Jan Olaf has been a member of faculty at the Niels Bohr Institute in Copenhagen.

Jens W. Moberg is the owner and founder of the consultancy and advisory firm Leadership Institute and serves as chairman of Grundfos, PostNord and Herlufsholm. He has more than 20 years of experience in executive positions in technology companies, including Microsoft, IBM and Better Place. From 2005 to 2008 he was head of Enterprise Partner Group at Microsoft USA and responsible for a turnover of 8 billion USD. As the highest placed Dane in the history of the company, Jens served as Corporate Vice President at Microsoft.

Jo Ashman is Scottish and spent most of his career in the travel and airline industry in the United Kingdom. He received his first managerial role for Scandinavian Airlines at the age of 30 and went on to hold several leadership positions until his retirement in 2011, as Country Sales Manager for the United Kingdom. For over 40 years he worked with numerous leaders from Norway, Sweden and Denmark, giving him a unique outside perspective on the Nordic leadership style.

Jón Baldvin Hannibalsson is a former Icelandic politician and diplomat. He financed his university studies at Edinburgh, Stockholm and Harvard as a trawler-fisherman during summers in the North Atlantic. Jón has been leader of Iceland's social democratic party and minister of finance and foreign affairs. He led the EEA-negotiations with the EU on Iceland's behalf and took the lead in soliciting support for the Baltic nations' restoration of independence. Finally, Jón is an honorary citizen of Vilnius.

Jon Krogh is a Danish adventurer and serial entrepreneur, most recently in tourism in Greenland. He sometimes supplements his own adventures with work in mainstream organizations like Tele-Post. He served as a sergeant in the Danish army and has led fundraising efforts for kids with troubled families. Jon grew up in New Zealand.

Jørgen Lindegaard is a prominent Danish business executive who has held several management and board positions in Danish and foreign companies. After more than 25 years in the telecommunications industry, he became the CEO of Scandinavian Airlines (SAS), where he oversaw a turbulent time in the aviation industry, including 9/11 and the deadly crash of SAS flight SK686 at Milan Linate on 8 October 2001. After returning the company to profitability, he left in 2006 to become the CEO of ISS, the world's largest facilities management company and Denmark's largest global employer. In 2006 he became Knight of 1st Degree of Dannebrog.

Kenneth Mikkelsen is a Danish writer, speaker, leadership adviser and organizational expert. He has published widely on issues of leadership and the shifting nature of business in the 21st century. Kenneth is a sought-after speaker and facilitates workshops globally on the future of work, neo-generalism, leadership and transformational learning. He is also co-author of the book *The Neo-Generalist* (2015) with Richard Martin. The book explores the value of multidisciplinarity, of living in more than one world. Further, he is founder of FutureShifts and an associate in the Drucker Society Europe and Copenhagen Institute for Futures Studies.

Kigge Hvid is the founding CEO of INDEX: Design to Improve Life®. Developing new concepts, testing them and implementing them are the hallmarks of her acclaimed work in leadership roles. Kigge has been a frequent panelist and theme-setter at forums around the world, and she is a member of the Danish Government's Disruption Council and of World Economic Forum's Expert Network. Kigge has been recognized as one of the world's leading advocates for "design to improve life" and was awarded an honorary doctorate in 2006 by the Art Center College of Design in Pasadena, California and in 2016 from University of Huddersfield.

Lars Tvede is a Danish entrepreneur and investor living in Switzerland. He is listed in The Guru Guide to Marketing as one of the world's 62 leading thinkers of marketing. Lars spent 11 years in portfolio management and investment banking before moving to the high-tech and telecommunications industries in the mid-1990s, where he was co-founder of several technology companies. He is the author of 15 books, which have been published in 11 languages. Lars holds a Master's degree in Engineering and a Bachelor's degree in International Commerce, and is a certified derivatives trader from National Futures Association in Chicago.

Lene Rachel Andersen is a Danish futurist, author, philosopher and publisher. She has written comedy and entertainment for Danish media and has spent considerable time in the US; she went there a Dane and returned a European. She has a BA in Business Economy and studied theology. For her work as a writer and a publisher she has received the Ebbe Kløvedal-Reich Democracy Baton (2007) and the Danish librarians' Døssing Prize.

Marco Sammicheli is a design curator based in Milan. He has curated several projects for public museums and private galleries in Italy and abroad and is dedicated to Bruno Munari, James Irvine, Ettore Sottsass, Gabriele De Vecchi, among others. He teaches at the Design School of Politecnico di Milano, and works as an essayist and a journalist. Marco has contributed to the 14th International Architecture Biennale in Venice and recently curated a residency at the Italian Embassy in Copenhagen.

Massimo Caiazza is Italian and the founding partner of Caiazza & Partners International Law-firm. He was the first foreign lawyer to be admitted to the Swedish Bar Association and the first foreign citizen to be admitted as "Advokat" in Sweden. Massimo is fluent in Italian, Swedish and English. He lives the ethics of the legal profession as an independent lawyer following both the Swedish and the Italian rules and code of conduct.

Melanie McCall is a British senior consultant for People & Performance, living in Copenhagen. She facilitates leadership development across a broad range of organizations and sectors. As Global Leadership Development Director for Carlsberg, Mel launched the group's first leadership training academy. She is a fellow of the British Chartered Institute of Personnel and Development (FCIPD) and has a 22-year background in HR with industry brand leaders in FMCG, financial services, retail, manufacturing and IT.

Mika Anttonen is the founder and principal shareholder of the Finnish energy company St1. He has years of experience in international fuel trade, the decentralized production of renewable energy and private entrepreneurship. Mika began his career as an entrepreneur in fuel trade and rapidly built up a diverse Nordic energy company which today pursues its vision to become a leading producer and seller of CO2-aware energy. The company is investing heavily in renewable energy research and production, ranging from industrial wind power to advanced biofuels and geothermal heat.

Mikael Kretz is a serial entrepreneur focusing on building global consultancy companies. He started his first company when he was 24 and after 5 years the company reached 100 employees and was sold to a public company in Sweden. His most recent endeavor, Qgroup, works with specialist brands in a variety of areas within technology and professional services. Qgroup was founded in 2012 and currently has 24 subsidiaries with offices around the world with more than 300 employees.

Morten Andersen is a Danish former NFL kicker. He is the all-time leader in games played and the all-time leading scorer in NFL history. In 2017, he was inducted into the Pro Football Hall of Fame. Since his retirement from football in 2008, Morten has worked with international business consulting, speaking and personal consultations. He has also established The Morten Andersen Family Foundation, a non-profit organization that raises money for quality of life programs for children and youth. The foundation also created a program which raises money to support critically wounded Special Operations soldiers and the families of the fallen.

Morten Ravn is Research Coordinator and Curator at the Viking Ship Museum in Roskilde. He has a PhD in Archaeology from the University of Copenhagen and has lectured on maritime and experimental archaeology at Universities in Denmark, Scotland and Croatia. Morten's career has involved large-scale digital recording of archaeological ship timbers, maritime heritage and research on Viking Age shipbuilding, seafaring and naval warfare. He has published numerous papers in both Danish and international journals, recently also the book *Viking Age War Fleets* (2016).

Niclas Carlsson is founder and CEO of Founders Alliance, a non-profit organization established in 2002. Founders Alliance is an entrepreneur collaborative forum comprised of 600 of Sweden's leading entrepreneurs. In 2015 he initiated the 1st Entrepreneurs World Summit, an annual forum for entrepreneurs across the globe. Niclas holds a Master's degree in Business Administration from Uppsala University in Sweden. He is also an endurance athlete having competed in several ultramarathons and adventure races. Niclas resides in Stockholm with his wife and three children.

Niels Dalhoff is a former elite Special Operations soldier from the Danish Jaeger Corps. With a business college degree and a Master's from Oxford Brooks University, he has subsequently worked as a management consultant, coach and trainer in leadership and organizational development. Besides having held senior management positions in Ørsted and Scandinavian Airlines, responsible for leadership and organizational development, Niels has worked as professional certified coach. Inspired by his training in the Special Forces, he has always been eager for adventure and has climbed mountains all over the world.

Patrick Trancu is an Italian corporate communications professional. He has spent the past 30 years advising multinational clients across industries on corporate communication strategies. For the past 15 years he has focused on crisis and issues management, including: managing terrorist threats, airline crashes, environmental/health issues, product contaminations, CEO deaths, plant closings and layoffs. He also advises clients on the design and implementation of crisis preparedness programs internationally.

Per Heggenes is the CEO of IKEA Foundation, the philanthropic arm of Stichting INGKA Foundation, the owner of the IKEA Group. As CEO, he sets and drives the Foundation's funding and innovation strategies and is a tireless advocate for children living in some of the world's poorest communities. Since becoming the Foundation's first CEO in 2009, Per has presided over the Foundation's evolution into global, grant-making philanthropy that funds programs in more than 45 countries.

Per Tryding is vice president at the Swedish Chamber of Commerce in Southern Sweden and an executive learning specialist. He is also a board member of Malmö University and MiL Foundation (Sweden), which works with leadership learning development. He has an MSc in International Business Administration (Lund University, Sweden) and a PhD (Aarhus

University, Denmark). In 2015 Per published *Lärande för ledarskap* ("Learning for leadership") on value adding in management training and development.

Pernille Hippe Brun is a management consultant and executive coach. She lives and works in both Copenhagen and San Francisco and advises organizations and leaders globally. Pernille has designed MBA programs on three continents. She is a pioneer in strength-based leadership and is co-author of the bestselling *Strengths-Based Leadership Handbook* (2016) together with management guru David Cooperrider.

Rasmus Stuhr Jakobsen is CEO for CARE in Denmark. He has previously worked for the United Nations World Food Programme, the Red Cross and the Danish Refugee Council. For almost a decade Rasmus worked with senior management in a multicultural environment, being responsible for responses to some of the world's largest humanitarian crises.

Roberto Maiorana is a Swedish/Italian business executive. He is the executive director of traffic management at the Swedish Transport Administration. Before joining the Transport Administration, he had a long career in Scandinavian Airlines. He started as an air steward and ended his airline career as CEO of SAS Ground Handling AB Sweden. During his career in Scandinavian Airlines, Roberto held a number of international positions, which gave him a unique perspective in working cross-culturally.

Rufus Gifford served as United States Ambassador to Denmark from 2013 to 2017. As Ambassador, his personal mission was to transform a historically great relationship to meet the challenges of the future by engaging Danes —especially younger Danes—on bilateral and global issues. Determined to modernize diplomacy and build back trust in institutions, he pursued a never-before-seen public diplomacy strategy, allowing cameras to document his life and his work. The award-winning documentary series titled "I am the Ambassador" was featured on Netflix and is currently being aired on television in over 10 countries. Rufus was knighted by the Queen of Denmark in January 2017.

Sakari Oramo is a Finnish conductor. He is the Chief Conductor of the BBC Symphony Orchestra as well as the Royal Stockholm Philharmonic Orchestra. For ten years he was the musical director of the City of Birmingham Symphony Orchestra, and after a decade as Chief Conductor of the Finnish Radio Symphony Orchestra, he has now serves as their honorary conductor.

Sanna Suvanto-Harsaae is a Nordic board professional. She is chairman of Altia OY, Footway AB, BoConcept AS, TCM AS, Best VPG AS, vice chair at Paulig Oyj, and member of the board at Scandinavian Airlines and Bromann group. Sanna is also part of the Corporate Governance faculty at Copenhagen Business School and she has previously been member of boards at Clas Ohlson AB, Duni AB, Symrise AG, among others. She has been Managing Director at Reckitt Benckiser, and European Marketing Director at Procter and Gamble and at Synoptik. Sanna is a Finnish and Danish citizen and graduated from Lund University.

Stefan Skantz's career in Scandinavian companies spans more than 30 years, first in Swedish Management Group and then in Scandinavian Airlines System. His primary focus has been within customer care and emergency response. Stefan's experience includes being responsible for the Special Assistance Team in the Emergency Response organization with more than 500 members and being deeply engaged in the handling of the SAS accident in Milan 2001 and the Spanair accident in Madrid 2008.

Thomas Pedersen co-founded OneLogin, Inc. and was the Chairman and Chief Technology Officer of the company until 2017. He has more than 15 years of experience in building and selling carrier-grade billing systems for phone companies, initially at Cisco-backed Digiquant in Denmark and later at Intec Telecom Systems in the US.

Vagn Sørensen is a Danish professional board chairman and member. He has had a long career in the aviation industry, including 17 years at Scandinavian Airlines, where he held the position of Executive Vice President and Deputy CEO until 2001. From 2001-06 he served as President and CEO at Austrian Airlines Group, including serving as the Chairman of the Association of European Airlines. Since then he has held numerous board positions with large international corporations, for example TDC Group, Air Canada, F L Smidth, Scandic Hotels AB, Royal Caribbean Cruise Line.

Vincent F. Hendricks is Professor of Formal Philosophy at the University of Copenhagen. He is director of the Center for Information and Bubble Studies (CIBS) sponsored by the Carlsberg Foundation. Vincent has been awarded a number of national and international prizes for his research, among them the Elite Research Prize by the Danish Ministry of Science, Technology and Innovation, the Roskilde Festival Elite Research Prize, the Rosenkjær Prize by the Danish Broadcasting Company, and the Choice Magazine Outstanding Title Award. Between 2005 and 2015 he was editor-in-chief of *Synthese* an international journal for epistemology, methodology and philosophy of science.

Åslaug Marie Haga is the Executive Director of the Global Crop Diversity Trust. She is a career diplomat, politician and private sector executive. Åslaug has held various positions in the Norwegian Ministry of Foreign Affairs, including in the Norwegian Mission to the United Nations in New York and the Embassy in New Delhi. She was politically appointed and held the position as State Secretary/Deputy Minister in the Ministry of Foreign Affairs from 1997-99. Åslaug has published three books—one novel and two books on Norwegian politics.

BIBLIOGRAPHY

Andersen, Lene Rachel, and Tomas Björkman. *The Nordic Secret. A European Story of Beauty and Freedom* (Fri Tanke, 2017).

Anonymous. *The Poetic Edda* (Oxford University Press, 2014, revised edition). Translated by Carolyne Larrington.

Barraclough, Eleanor Rosamund. *Beyond the Northlands: Viking Voyages and the Old Norse Sagas* (Oxford University Press, 2016).

Bartlett, Christopher A., Kenton W. Elderkin and Barbara Feinberg. "Jan Carlzon: CEO at SAS (A)", *Harvard Business School Case* 392-149 (June 1993, revised edition).

Booth, Michael. *The Almost Nearly Perfect People: Behind the Myth of Scandinavian Utopia* (Vintage, 2015).

Brafman, Ori, and Rod A. Beckstrom. *The Starfish and the Spider: The Unstoppable Power of Leaderless Organizations* (Portfolio, 2007).

Brafman, Ori, and Judah Pollack. *The Chaos Imperative: How Chance and Disruption Increase Innovation, Effectiveness, and Success* (Piatkus, 2013).

Brun, Pernille Hippe, David Cooperrider and Mikkel Ejsing. *Strengths-Based Leadership Handbook* (Crown Custom Publishing, 2016).

Calvino, Italo. *Six Memos for the Next Millennium* (Penguin, 2009). Translated by Patrick Creagh.

Carlzon, Jan. *Moments of Truth* (Ballinger Publishing, 1987).

Castells, Manuel. *Networks of Outrage and Hope: Social Movements in the Internet Age* (Polity, 2015, 2nd edition).

Collins, Isabel. "The Ambassador of Denmark on Danish Culture and *All That We Share*", *Belonging Works* (March 2017). https://belongingworks.com/2017/03/06/the-ambassador-of-denmark-on-danish-culture-and-all-that-we-share/

Csikszentmihalyi, Mihalyi. *Creativity: The Psychology of Discovery and Invention* (Harper Perennial, 2013).

Dehnugara, Khurshed. *Flawed but Willing: Leading Organisations in the Age of Connection* (LID, 2014).

D'Souza, Steven, and Diana Renner. *Not Knowing: The Art of Turning Uncertainty into Opportunity* (LID, 2014).

Duckworth, Angela. *Grit: The Power of Passion and Perseverance* (Vermilion, 2016).

Falkvinge, Rick. *Swarmwise: The Tactical Manual to Changing the World* (CreateSpace Publishing, 2013). http://falkvinge.net/files/2013/04/Swarmwise-2013-by-Rick-Falkvinge-v1.1-2013Sep01.pdf

Ferrante, Elena. *Frantumaglia: A Writer's Journey* (Europa Editions, 2016). Translated by Ann Goldstein.

Fukuyama, Francis. *The Origins of Political Order: From Prehuman Times to the French Revolution* (Farrar, Straus and Giroux, 2011).

Gaiman, Neil. *Norse Mythology* (Bloomsbury, 2017).

Gleiser, Marcelo. *The Simple Beauty of the Unexpected: A Natural Philosopher's Quest for Trout and the Meaning of Everything* (ForeEdge, 2016).

Goldin, Ian, and Chris Kutarna. *Age of Discovery: Navigating the Risk and Rewards of Our New Renaissance* (Bloomsbury, 2016).

Grant, Adam. *Give and Take: A Revolutionary Approach to Success* (Viking Books, 2013).

Gray, Dave, with Thomas Vander Wal. *The Connected Company* (O'Reilly, 2012).

Greenleaf, Robert K. *The Servant as Leader* (Center for Applied Studies, 1973).

Handy, Charles. *The Age of Unreason* (Arrow, 2002).

Handy, Charles. *The Empty Raincoat* (Arrow, 2002).

Handy, Charles. *The Second Curve: Thoughts on Reinventing Society* (Random House, 2015).

Helfand, Jessica. *Design: The Invention of Desire* (Yale University Press, 2016).

Hendricks, Vincent F., and Pelle G. Hansen. *Infostorms: Why Do We "Like"? Explaining Individual Behavior on the Social Net* (Springer, 2016, 2nd edition).

Hlupic, Vlatka. *The Management Shift: How to Harness the Power of People and Transform Your Organization for Sustainable Success* (Palgrave Macmillan, 2014).

Høeg, Peter. *Smilla's Sense of Snow* (Picador, 2012). Translated by T. Nunnally.

Hofstede, Geert, Gert Jan Hofstede and Michael Minkov. *Cultures and Organizations: Software of the Mind* (McGraw-Hill, 2010, 3rd edition).

Hustvedt, Siri. *Living, Thinking, Looking* (Sceptre, 2013).

Hyde, Lewis. *The Gift: Creativity and the Artist in the Modern World* (Vintage, 2007, 2nd edition).

Jensen, Rolf, and Mika Aaltonen. *The Renaissance Society: How the Shift from Dream Society to the Age of Individual Control Will Change the Way You Do Business* (McGraw-Hill, 2013).

Jesch, Judith. "Constructing the Warrior Ideal in the Late Viking Age", in Lena Holmquist and Michael Olausson (eds.), *The Martial Society: Aspects of Warriors, Fortifications and Social Change in Scandinavia* (Archaeological Research Laboratory, Stockholm University, 2009), pp. 71-78.

Johansen, Bob. *Leaders Make the Future: Ten New Leadership Skills for an Uncertain World* (Berrett–Koehler, 2012, 2nd edition).

Jónsdóttir, Birgitta. "Democracy in the Digital Era", *New Internationalist* (January 2015). https://newint.org/features/2015/01/01/democracy-digital-era-keynote/

Kerr, James. *Legacy: 15 Lessons in Leadership* (Constable, 2013).

Kilpi, Esko (ed.). *Perspectives on New Work: Exploring Emerging Conceptualizations* (Sitra, 2016). https://media.sitra.fi/2017/02/28142631/Selvityksia114.pdf

Kingsley, Patrick. *How to be Danish: A Journey to the Cultural Heart of Denmark* (Short Books, 2013).

Knausgaard, Karl Ove. *A Death in the Family: My Struggle, Book 1* (Vintage, 2014). Translated by Don Bartlett.

Kolind, Lars, and Jacob Bøtter. *Unboss* (Jyllands-Postens Forlag, 2012).

Lakey, George. *Viking Economics: How the Scandinavians Got It Right—And We Can, Too* (Melville House Publishing, 2016).

Larsen, Henrik Holt, and Ulla Bruun de Neergaard. *Nordic Lights: A Research Project on Nordic Leadership and Leadership in the Nordic Countries* (Copenhagen Business School, 2007). http://www.kl.dk/ImageVaultFiles/id_34172/cf_202/Nordic_Light.PDF

Leski, Kyna. *The Storm of Creativity* (MIT Press, 2015).

Levene, Rick, Christopher Locke, Doc Searls and David Weinberger. *The Cluetrain Manifesto: The End of Business as Usual* (Basic Books, 2011).

Madsbjerg, Christian. *Sensemaking: What Makes Human Intelligence Essential in the Age of the Algorithm* (Little, Brown, 2017).

Madsen, Helle Bruun. "Den skandinaviske ledelsesstil lever i bedste velgående", *Lederne* (July 2017). https://www.lederne. dk/presse-og-nyheder/nyheder/den-skandinaviske-ledelsess-til-lever-i-bedste-velgaaende

Martin, Richard. "Ready to Jump: Agile, Teams and Autonomy in the Peloton", *Hack and Craft News* (November 2016). http://hncnews.com/ready-jump-agile-teams-autonomy-peleton

McConnell, Jane. *The Organization in the Digital Age* (NetJMC, 2016). http://www.organization-digital-age.com

Meyer, Claus. *The Nordic Kitchen: One Year of Family Cooking* (Mitchell Beazley, 2016).

Meyer, Erin. *The Culture Map: Breaking Through the Invisible Boundaries of Global Business* (PublicAffairs, 2014).

Mikkelsen, Kenneth. "Seeing the World with Fresh Eyes," *Global Peter Drucker Forum Blog* (November 2016). https://www.druckerforum.org/blog/?p=1404

Mikkelsen, Kenneth, and Richard Martin. *The Neo-Generalist: Where You Go Is Who You Are* (LID, 2016).

Moore, Alan. *Do Design: Why Beauty is Key to Everything* (Do Book Company, 2016).

Naylor, Max. *Viking Expansion.* Map. (Wikipedia Commons, located 6 March 2018 at: https://en.wikipedia.org/wiki/Viking_expansion).

Needham, Alex. "Sakari Oramo to Become BBC Symphony Orchestra Chief Conductor", *The Guardian* (23 February 2012). https://www.theguardian.com/music/2012/feb/23/sakari-oramo-bbcso-chief-conductor

Nielsen, Poul. *Working Life in the Nordic Region: Challenges and Proposals* (Nordisk Ministerråd, 2016). http://norden.diva-portal.org/smash/get/diva2:934717/FULLTEXT01.pdf

Noë, Alva. *Strange Tools: Art and Human Nature* (Hill and Wang, 2016).

Nordic Council of Ministers. *Nordic Statistics* (Nordic Council of Ministers, 2016). http://norden.diva-portal.org/smash/get/diva2:1040725/FULLTEXT03.pdf

Pagel, Mark. *Wired for Culture: The Natural History of Human Cooperation* (Penguin, 2013).

Parker, Philip. *The Northmen's Fury: A History of the Viking World* (Vintage, 2015).

Partanen, Anu. *The Nordic Theory of Everything: In Search of a Better Life* (HarperCollins, 2016).

Pontefract, Dan. *The Purpose Effect: Building Meaning in Yourself, Your Role, and Your Organization* (Elevate, 2016).

Porter, Michael E., and Scott Stern with Michael Green. *Social Progress Index 2017* (Social Progress Imperative, 2017). http://www.socialprogressindex.com/assets/downloads/resources/en/English-2017-Social-Progress-Index-Findings-Report_embargo-d-until-June-21-2017.pdf

Pringle, Heather. "New Visions of the Vikings", *National Geographic* (March 2017), pp. 30-51. http://www.nationalgeographic.com/magazine/2017/03/vikings-ship-burials-battle-reenactor/

Pye, Michael. *The Edge of the World: How the North Sea Made Us Who We Are* (Penguin, 2015).

Ravn, Morten. *Viking Age War Fleets: Shipbuilding, Resource Management and Maritime Warfare in 11th-Century Denmark* (Viking Ship Museum, 2016).

Rehn, Alf. *Dangerous Ideas: When Provocative Thinking is Your Most Valuable Asset* (BookBaby, 2013). http://dangerousideas.strikingly.com

Rushkoff, Douglas. *Throwing Rocks at the Google Bus: How Growth Became the Enemy of Prosperity* (Portfolio Penguin, 2016).

Russell, Helen. *The Year of Living Danishly: Uncovering the Secrets of the World's Happiest Country* (Icon Books, 2016).

Rycker, Sonali De. "Why Supercell's founder wants to be the world's least powerful CEO. Secrets from the frontline", *Medium* (May 2017). https://medium.com/accel-insights/why-supercells-founder-wants-to-be-the-world-s-least-powerful-ceo-38bf173d607c

Saint-Exupéry, Antoine de. *The Little Prince* (Egmont, 2009). Translated by Katherine Woods.

Schumacher, E. F. *Small is Beautiful: A Study of Economics as if People Mattered* (Vintage, 2011).

Schwab, Klaus. "The Fourth Industrial Revolution: What It Means and How to Respond", *Foreign Affairs* (December 2015). https://www.foreignaffairs.com/articles/2015-12-12/fourth-industrial-revolution

Sennett, Richard. *Together: The Rituals, Pleasures and Politics of Co-operation* (Penguin, 2013).

Shepherd, Nan. *The Living Mountain* (Canongate, 2011).

Simonyi, András, and Debra L. Cagan (eds.). *Nordic Ways* (Center for Transatlantic Relations, Johns Hopkins University, 2016).

Sinek, Simon. *Leaders Eat Last: Why Some Teams Pull Together and Others Don't* (Portfolio Penguin, 2014).

Social Progress Imperative (located 6 March 2018 at http://www.socialprogressimperative.org/)

Social Progress Index (located 6 March 2018 at https://www.socialprogressindex.com/methodology)

Solnit, Rebecca. *Hope in the Dark: Untold Histories, Wild Possibilities* (Haymarket Books, 2016, 3rd edition).

Somerville, Angus A., and R. Andrew McDonald. *The Viking Age: A Reader* (Toronto University Press, 2010).

Sørensen, Lars Rebien. "Fighting Diabetes in the 21st century", *Harvard Business Review* (December 2015). https://hbr.org/2015/12/fighting-diabetes-in-the-21st-century

Stadil, Christian, and Lene Tanggaard. *In the Shower with Picasso: Sparking Your Creativity and Imagination* (LID, 2014).

Steele, Tom. *Knowledge is Power! The Rise and Fall of European Popular Education Movements, 1848-1939* (Peter Lang, 2007).

Strauss, Mark. "Discovery Could Rewrite History of Vikings in New World", *National Geographic* (March 2016). http://news.nationalgeographic.com/2016/03/160331-viking-discovery-north-america-canada-archaeology/

Strid, Steve, and Claes Andréasson. *The Viking Manifesto: The Scandinavian Approach to Business and Blasphemy* (Marshall Cavendish, 2007).

Sturluson, Snorri. *The Prose Edda* (Penguin, 2005). Translated by Jesse L. Byock.

Thomsen, Steen. *Industrial Foundations in the Danish Economy* (Center for Corporate Governance, Copenhagen Business School, 2013). http://www.tifp.dk/wp-content/uploads/2011/11/Industrial-Foundations-and-Danish-Society1.pdf

Thomsen. Steen. "Industrial Foundations—The Danish Model", in András Simonyi and Debra L. Cagan (eds.), *Nordic Ways* (Center for Transatlantic Relations, Johns Hopkins University, 2016), pp. 81-87.

Truitt, E. R. "Fantasy North", *Aeon* (February 2016). https:// aeon.co/essays/what-lies-beneath-the-ice-of-our-fascination-with-the-north

Tvede, Lars. "Decentralization," *LinkedIn* (April 2017). https:// www.linkedin.com/pulse/decentralization-tvede-lars

Tvede, Lars. *The Creative Society: How the Future Can Be Won* (LID, 2016, 2nd edition).

Weinberger, David. *Small Pieces Loosely Joined: A Unified Theory of the Web* (Basic Books, 2003).

Weinstein, Arnold. *Northern Arts: The Breakthrough of Scandinavian Literature and Art, from Ibsen to Bergman* (Princeton University Press, 2011).

Wheatley, Margaret J. *Finding Our Way: Leadership for an Uncertain Time* (Berrett–Koehler, 2007).

Wheatley, Margaret J. *Leadership and the New Science: Discovering Order in a Chaotic World* (Berrett–Koehler, 1999, 2nd edition).

Whitman, Walt. *The Complete Poems* (Penguin, 2004).

Wood, James, and Karl Ove Knausgaard. "Writing My Struggle: An Exchange", The Paris Review 211 (Winter 2014). https:// www.theparisreview.org/miscellaneous/6345/writing-emmy-struggle-em-an-exchange-james-wood-karl-ove-knausgaard

Worrall, Simon. "How Much Viking Lore Is True?" *National Geographic* (January 2017). http://news.nationalgeographic. com/2017/01/viking-beyond-northlands-norse-saga-barra-clough/

FILMOGRAPHY

Detailed reference is made to several films in the text of *Return of the Vikings*.

Babettes gæstebud (Babette's Feast)
Year of release: 1987.
Director: Gabriel Axel.
Screenplay: Gabriel Axel, based on a short story by Karen Blixen written under the pseudonym of Isak Dinesen.

Collaboration: On the Edge of a New Paradigm?
Year of release: 2014.
Directors: Katja Gry Birkegaard Carlsen and Alfred Birkegaard Hansted.
Created as part of Alfred Birkegaard Hansted's PhD in Philosophy.
https://vimeo.com/119101747

Det sjunde inseglet (The Seventh Seal)
Year of release: 1957.
Director: Ingmar Bergman.
Screenplay: Ingmar Bergman.

En man som heter Ove (A Man Called Ove)
Year of release: 2015.
Director: Hannes Holm.
Screenplay: Hannes Holm, based on a novel by Fredrik Backman.

Hrútar (Rams)
Year of release: 2015.
Director: Grímur Hákonarson.
Screenplay: Grímur Hákonarson.

Kauas pilvet karkaavat (Drifting Clouds)
Year of release: 1996.
Director: Aki Kaurismäki.
Screenplay: Aki Kaurismäki

Mitt liv som hund (My Life as a Dog)
Year of release: 1985.
Director: Lasse Hallström.
Screenplay: Lasse Hallström, Reidar Jönsson, Brasse Brännström and Per Berglund, based on a novel by Reidar Jönsson.

Brief reference is also made to the following television series:

Borgen
Broadcast years: 2010–13
Creator: Adam Price

Bron/Broen (The Bridge)
Broadcast years: 2011–
Creator: Hans Rosenfeldt

Forbrydelsen (The Killing)
Broadcast years: 2007–12
Creator: Søren Sveistrup

ANNEX:
THE INSIDE–OUTSIDE
PERSPECTIVE

While the interviews that inform the content of *Return of the Vikings* were free-wheeling and wide-ranging, a few core questions provided shape and consistency to the conversations. The authors addressed these questions themselves during the course of researching the book.

WHAT DOES NORDIC LEADERSHIP MEAN TO YOU?

Henrik Jeberg
It boils down to three things: mutual trust, openness and low power distance. Having worked in a dozen countries on four continents, my experience is that these are the most distinguishing elements that differentiate Nordic-led companies from everyone else. In Nordic society, trust is a given until you prove yourself unworthy of it. In other cultures, the reverse is true, with people having to earn trust.

This one factor goes some way to explaining how the Nordics have developed wealthy, socially responsible and peaceful countries over the last century. If people are predominantly honest, you can get by with fewer corporate and public-sector overheads. There is a lower requirement for control, reviews, audits and so on. This means you can concentrate your efforts on the "outliers" instead. It also lowers the thresholds for doing business with new customers and vendors, making it easier to hire new employees, and smoothing the interaction with government institutions.

Openness and low power distance enables information to flow in any direction in an organization. Managers tend to share extensive information about the company's strategy, goals and plans, and workers feel able to point out mistakes and inefficiencies without fear of recrimination. In some cultures, such action can jeopardize jobs and livelihood.

Chris Shern

Trust. I found Massimo Caiazza's comparison between Italy and Sweden compelling. He explained that in Italy it is all about the family because that is who you can trust, whereas in the Nordics, trust is woven into the social fabric, meaning that people trust the institutions and the system too. In many countries, you must build the relationships before you start talking business. In the Nordics, you can dive straight in, addressing issues and negotiating.

Consensus. This is about making sure everyone is on board, heading in the same direction, and feeling included and heard. This was my personal experience when I worked for Scandinavian Airlines. I grew to appreciate the practice having initially been frustrated by it, discovering that time invested in securing buy-in and alignment tended to be less than the time required to fix problems created by a rush to action.

Sweden has the nickname "consensus Sweden", but making sure everyone is heard is certainly a Nordic trait. In many cases, the role of leader is a facilitative one, making sure that everyone is in some way a part of the process.

Low power distance. The necessity to be heard or have an opinion in Nordic leadership became even more evident to me when I was working in Italy. I would prepare my team for when people visited from the Swedish head office, coaching them to share their opinion, to challenge, question and contribute. It was something that did not come naturally to my Italian colleagues, and I have noted similar reticence to speak up in the workplace among Americans and Asians.

Organizational structures are shallow in Nordic companies. Access to the leadership is completely normal. In fact, I have found all my so-called bosses to be more sparring partner than the person telling me what to do. They always managed to create a sense that we were "in this together".

Visionary. Many Nordic organizations, especially the business foundations, have a long-term, purpose-driven approach. Many of the Nordic leaders I have worked with, many of the people I have interviewed for this book, give the impression that they are contributing to a greater purpose.

Egalitarian. In a Nordic organization, nobody is better than anyone else, they just have different roles. This comes back to the topic of trust. The compensation structure of businesses in the Nordics has none of the anomalies and disparities between senior executives and other staff that are evident in other countries like the United States.

Communicative. The Nordic peoples are not known for their strong communication skills—certainly not the Finns or the Icelanders. But there are many different aspects to communication, and one key aspect is the ability to listen. That Jan Carlzon invested more than 50% of his time communicating, not only sharing the corporate vision but listening to the people, says it all really.

WHAT PERSONAL VALUES DO YOU SUBSCRIBE TO OR APPLY IN YOUR LIFE?

Henrik Jeberg
Integrity, respect, work ethics, courage.

Chris Shern
Freedom, influence, adventure.

WHAT FACTORS DO YOU FEEL HAVE INFLUENCED NORDIC LEADERSHIP?

Henrik Jeberg
The climate has a lot to do with it. The harsh realities of living in the Nordics in ancient times forced us to work together in teams to survive winter and thrive. We needed to plan ahead in order to collect enough food to see us through the winter. We were forced to rely on others as no one could survive on their own.

With limited natural resources, we have had to rely on trade, shipping and innovation to make our way in a global context.

So, you could argue that knowledge-intensive trades have been intrinsic to our economy at an earlier stage than has been the case for many other countries.

Chris Shern

Climate. This is so harsh and volatile that you must be prepared for anything, being adaptable, ready to change plans at a moment's notice. There is also a spiritual element, with the natural world providing a constant reminder that there is a power greater than you.

Size. These are small countries. They are characterized by something of an underdog mentality, but are noted for punching above their weight, as President Obama put it. Dating from the Viking era, the Nordic peoples have followed the urge to head out into the world and explore, demonstrating leadership and an appetite for risk. The odds are there to be overcome.

Limited natural resources. This has generated an appreciation of what you do have, and innovative ways of using it. But also the catalyst for seeking your fortune overseas, adventuring and exploring.

Homogeneity. When everyone is from the same tribe it makes it a bit easier to trust everyone, easier to lead and easier to follow. There is a downside to this, as I am reminded of frequently as an American in Copenhagen. Even though I speak the language fluently, have held high positions in Nordic organizations, am a member of a strong professional and personal network, and am married to a Dane, I will always be an outsider. Americans tend to assimilate, whereas Nordics are known for forming strong expat communities, even as they interact effectively with other cultures.

IS NORDIC LEADERSHIP EXPORTABLE? WHAT ARE THE RISKS?

Henrik Jeberg

I believe some of the values and ideas can be exported and uti-lized successfully in certain types of companies. An example would include knowledge-intensive companies like the high-tech start-ups found in Silicon Valley. I am not convinced it would work on a Chinese construction site or in an Indian tex-tiles workshop. Not without significant cultural change.

It makes no sense to apply the Nordic leadership model with-out personal autonomy in the workplace. If the individual is not enabled to make decisions for themselves on behalf of the com-pany, the idea of openness and trust will be vacuous—nothing more than meaningless words.

Chris Shern

In principle, Nordic leadership is exportable. After all, who does not want to feel respected and trusted? Who does not want to follow a leader who is driven by a greater purpose?

However, the elements we have identified as being character-istic of Nordic leadership have to be adapted to the national or organization culture that you are in. It is self-evident that one size does not fit all. In reality, some companies in other cultures are so lacking in trust that it would take a major organizational transformation to be able to lead effectively in the Nordic style. In the wrong context, an authentic, values-driven person who trusts others and adopts a collaborative approach to business could flounder and be taken advantage of. There is always the danger that the promotion of consensus is misunderstood as a sign of weakness or indecision.

WHAT DOES THE VIKING HERITAGE MEAN TO YOU?

Henrik Jeberg

The more I study it, the more I see how much of our Nordic values stem from the Viking era rather than the social democracies that emerged in the 1950s.

At a time where traditional religion is losing its importance in Northern Europe—even blamed for many contemporary global ills—I think many people are becoming increasingly interested in "the Old Ways". In general, the Viking heritage does not replace religion, but it does provide a "tribal" feeling, a sense of belonging.

Chris Shern

My ancestors come from Norway, Russia, the Netherlands, Ireland—all of them areas that were occupied by the Vikings. There is always the possibility that my DNA is 100% Viking!

Working on the book and living in Scandinavia has made me more aware of and interested in the Vikings and their legacy but it was not something I was attuned to growing up. One of my grandfathers was proud of his Norwegian heritage but it was my Russian grandparents, who were immigrants to the United States, who exerted more of an influence on my life at a young age.

The Viking virtues represent a particularly strong draw for me. I find them highly relevant to navigating the times of extreme change that now confront us.

HOW DO YOU DEAL WITH UNCERTAINTY?

Henrik Jeberg

Life is uncertain—and becoming more so. Old paradigms are crumbling, and long-established worldviews are proven wrong every day. A strong values-based foundation is the best defense in a changing world. Knowing who you are, and what is important to you, helps you maintain your integrity as a human being, no matter what life throws at you.

Chris Shern

I find uncertainty normal. That does not mean, however, that I throw myself aimlessly into risk, or find uncertainty easy to deal with. I will always evaluate the potential consequences of the decisions I make and keep the interests of all those affected in mind.

ABOUT THE AUTHORS

 **Chris Shern** is a cultural adventurer. He has lived and worked internationally for over 20 years. Chris was employed by Scandinavian Airlines for many years in a variety of leadership roles across three continents. Currently, he is Managing Director of International Management Education (IME), a Danish non-profit foundation specializing in leadership development. Chris also works as a business consultant. Raised in the US Midwest, Chris now lives in Copenhagen with his wife and two adult children.

https://www.linkedin.com/in/chrisshern/

 **Henrik Jeberg** has worked in the international IT sector for over 25 years. He has lived in Europe, Asia, Australia and the US. Henrik was part of the top-management of Navision Software, which was sold to Microsoft. He later became Deputy Director General of the Danish

Ministry of Finance, leading the Government's horizontal IT complex. Henrik currently works as a mergers-and-acquisitions advisor, and serves as President of the Danish–American Chamber of Commerce in California where he lives with his family.

https://www.linkedin.com/in/henrikjeberg/

Richard Martin is a freelance writer and editor. He is the co-author of *The Neo-Generalist* and author of *Mean Streets and Raging Bulls*. He lives in Whitstable in the UK.

https://indalogenesis.com/about/

CPSIA information can be obtained
at www.ICGtesting.com
Printed in the USA
LVHW030338041218
599172LV00001B/89/P